MALAGA

GRANADA

SEVILLA

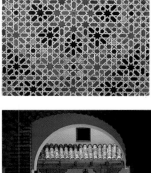

CORDOBA

ANDALUCIA

ANDALUCIA

When one isn't born in Andalusia, one has the opportunity to get to know it from the outside, and discover it bit by bit without being momentarily dazzled and without superficial enthusia. One can approach it cautiously, conscious of its seductive power. But its rich, fertil, old and wise soil, fertilized for the centuries by its serene soul changes to a welcoming ground where any roots can be transplanted.

It is the southern part of this bull's hide which is Spain. That is to say that it is more or less some 20% of the total area of Spain, a bit more than that ot its population and production, but a little less in its weath. It is as big as Portugal or Switzerland. It is as wide as Mother Earth, as loving, sweet, and generous.

Nowadays we try to simplify everything and so we divide it into the upper and lower parts, the easthern and western parts, the mountains and the lowlands and thus make new generalzations to describe it in a stroke. But this isn't easy to do, because its diversity is so wide that we can't simplify it. Moreover, the traditional Andalusia, the famous Andalusia of the great towns with their rich histories, is more universally known than the "other" Andalusia, the out of the way towns and villages which are the more authentic and intimate. The towns with treasures inherited from the centuries are the most surprising and varied and are frequently unknown by Andalucians themselves. Everyone knows about the Hams of Jabugo, but few people know of the mosque of Almonaster, a true jewel which is only a few litres of gasoline distant. Nor do many know of the village of Niebla or the Sierra de Líbar. The white villages on the mountains of Ronda alone are an enviable source of touristic wealth that many would like for themselves. How many Andalusians know the Alpujarras? And of these, how many know Darrícal or Lucainena, only a few steps from Ugíjar? And if, as the expression goes, Paris is worth a mass, then, Darrical is worth a journey. The port of Ragua is sorrounded by an idyllic view, complete with a little island in the the desert of Almería. The castle of Vélez-Blanco is as unknow as the "La Calahorra", only 9 kilometres from Guadix. Ubeda and Baeza have more charm than most Spanish provincial capitals. For a contrast to Doñana are the mountains of Segura and Cazorla. They are two nature reserves which are valuble for far more than their ecological conservation. Aracena, Palos, Osuna, Montoro, Baena, Cabra, Alcalá, Baza, Tabernas, Almuñécar, and a long list of lothers form a rosary of villages and towns which mirror the rich heritage and contain examples of Andalusian life.

Edilux

EDICION: Edilux. J.Agustin Nuñez Guarde. DIRECCION Y FOTOGRAFIA: Miguel Román Vega. COORDINACION: José Fernández Echevarría. DISEÑO Y MAQUETACION Y DIBUJOS:Taller de diseño. FOTOMECANICA: Infosag,S.A.

IMPRESION: Mateu Cromo, S.A. I.S.B.N.: 84-87282-61-X
DEPOSITO LEGAL: M. 15.401-1994

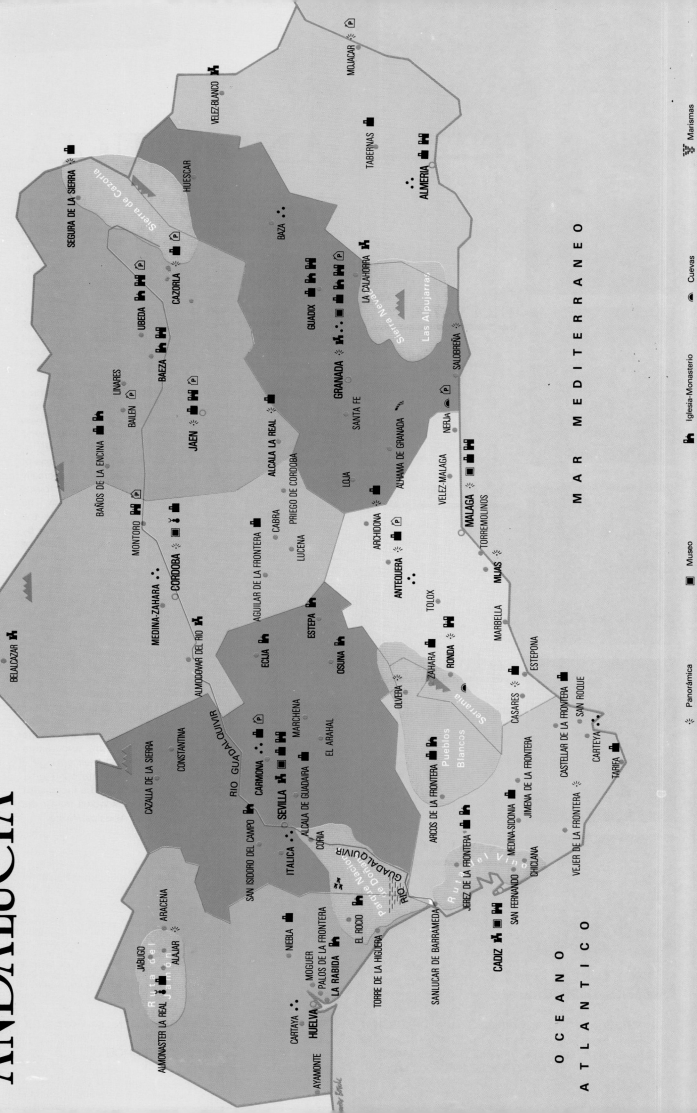

Pueblo de los verdiales
quien te pudiera tener

cosío en la faltriquera
como un pliego de papel

MALAGA

Traigo caballos y reyes
y la manilla de copas
para desplegar mi higuera
por la cortina del Muelle (El Piyayo)

T*he traveller who approaches Málaga, and perceives it in the distance; from the just crowned hill, from the bend just taken or from the window of the aeroplane, is overcome by that overwhelming sensation of ecstasy, that is experienced before the extraordinary, at the natural beauties. The blue of the sea, matched by that of the sky. The white of the foam which smooth waves form whimsically when caressing the silvered sands of the beaches. The green of the sugar-cane plantations and the ochre of the fertile lands, which, framed by the steep mountains that surround them, form a sight whose contemplation strongly attracts those, who have the privilege of seeing it sometime.*

It is a beautiful landscape which favourably predisposes one before arriving. And without any doubt this premonition comes true, because the Málaga people are as kind and welcoming as their landscape. The Malagueños' character resembles their enviroment: soft and kind, without earthquakes, nor typhoons. Without hardly any torrential rains, nor snowfalls. They are people of serene spirits, peaceful extroverts with a deep sense of humour, that without pretending to be witty, or becoming boring always know intuitively how to find the humorous side of things. Style that with kindness and subtle fun, they transmit to other people, no matter where re they come from. Those who feel alone in Málaga, feel alone because they wish it.

Málaga is known as the land of joy. It is not surprising the fact that millions of travellers, from all over the world, come here to spend their holidays, away from their daily work; and neither is it surprising that many of them come again, and some even settle down here to live in this welcoming oasis of tranquility, beauty and splendid climate.

3

EL PUERTO

The History of Málaga starts with the Phoenicians when these intrepid sailors and merchants, coming from what is now the Lebanon, established here a fish-salting centre, and a point of trade with the indigenous.

The Carthaginians passed through, but like all warlike people, they destroyed more than they built, and with the exception of some places named by them, little or nothing is left of this period. It is said that Mar-Habel, a captain of Hanibal, founded, at a certain point of the coast, a training camp. This camp, named after him, is today Marbella.

From Roman times there is an important archaelogical testimony; the ruins of an amphitheatre, (so called by the Malagueños), which was buried under rubbish for centuries and was unearthed in recent times, and is placed at the foot of the Alcazaba.

But of the many nations, that with more or less permanent character, passed through Málaga, the most impor-

tant were the Moslems, who established themselves in Spain in the name of the Caliph of Damascus. Later on Spain became independant, and in 1301 was fractioned in several different kingdoms, Málaga being one of them. At a later date it joined the powerful Nazarite Kingdom of Granada. In 1487 after hard fighting captained, at the Alcazaba, by the courageous Hammet el Zegri, Málaga surrendered to the Catholic Kings, Fernando and Isabel, after a very long siege.

The Christian period up to our days, is in ,neral, one of economical development during which Málaga harbour acquired a great importance with considerable merchandise and passenger traffic. Of this stage of development the second half of the 20th. century is the most important, in which, due to the increase of air transport, Málaga becomes the second city in Andalucía, the capital of one of the most important tourist areas in the world.

Gibralfaro

There are in Málaga and its province a great many interesting places to visit. We cannot mention them all here, since our purpose is to select the most known. When writing about Málaga, as well as about other provinces of that gigantic museum that is Spain, the problem that arises, is not what to say, but what to leave out.

LA CATEDRAL
(The Cathedral)

It is an interesting religious building in which a varied selection of different syles can be admired.

This variety of styles is due to the fact that the works were suspended on different occasions. With the passing of time, the tastes of the people as well as the architectonic decorative and artistic styles changed. Every time the work was resumed the craftsmen reflected on it the new tastes, the new tendencies.

Reconquered the city in 1487, several projects to elect a site were analysed. It was decided to build the temple on the site formerly occupied by the city's Moslem mosque.

In 1588 the works were suspended, and the already built part was inaugurated.

In 1783 the 93 ms. high, north tower was finished, and the works interrupted once again.

Wars, epidemics, change of ideas and people, lack of money, are the main causes of these suspensións, and also accounts for the variety of styles, detrimental to the unity, —that, indeed, contributes to making the temple polyfacetic, transforming it into an authentical museum of art history.

In the square facing the Cathedral on the north side, one finds the Episcopal Palace of classic structure and baroque decorations. It was started by Ramos, and finished by Martin de Aldehuela.

One of the towers originally designed is still incomplete.

The main façade, of Renaissance style, presents three enormous doors, over which we find three sculptures. The central of the Anunciation, to which all the building is de-

dicated; the other two represent St. Ciriac, and St. Paula. We can also observe on the façade something unmistakably Baroque, two, so called, salomonic columns which, like large twisted ships' ropes, give us an indication of the main feature of this dynamic 17th. century Italian style, which will substitute the more static Renaissance.

Each of the three great doors gives access to a different nave. In the centre there is the Choir, which cuts the panoramic vision, preventing us to see all the length of the nave.

The other two, free form any obstacles join up at the head with a half circle, called «girola or deambulatorio» (ambulatory) characteristic of all gothic churches; the style originally intended for the temple. There are many churches of this type in the south of Spain, and the expression, «andalusian canonic temple» has been used by many scholars.

To visit the inside one can start with the choir, on the outside of which, at the back, and facing the great doors, is exhibited, over a small altar, a sculpture in white marble; La Pietá, dated in the transition period of late 18th centuries. It is an important piece by the Pissani brothers. The most interesting; the classic central triangle, and the attitudes and expressions distorted by suffering, which shows us the baroque feeling the sculptors put into it.

Inside the choir, and carved in cedar wood, there are over a hundred figures, which represent venerable Church personages. The artists, Vargas, Alfaro and Mena, specially this last one, are authentical masters in wood carving, —very popular in Spain, where, fortunately, unlike in other countries it was never substituted for marble.

After visiting the choir, one can walk around the inside of the temple, visiting the two side naves, flanked by chapels, inside which abundant artistic objects of different styles are kept. We shall mention the most important among them.

Beginning with the south nave, the one of the incomplete tower, the first chapel is «Los Caidos», (The Fallen), with a Christ carving by Montañés, and a Mena «La Dolo rosa», (Our Lady of Sorrows).

La Alcazaba ➤

An Alonso Cano painting, of «La Virgen del Rosario», (Our Lady of the Rosary), is on show in the third chapel. One can feel the tenderness conveyed by the artist, a man of emotional sensual character, a fugitive, but also a repentant sinner; one of the great masters of religious painting, and who was able to transmit to his master pieces the best of his feelings.

La «Inmaculada», or la «Purísima», (The Immaculate), is found in the fourth chapel, with a baroque wooden retable.

The following space, or fifth chapel, is occupied by the door called, «Del Sol», (Sun Door), impressive, because of the finish and the quality of the wood, imported from South America.

In front of it, on the North side of the temple, there is a side door, called, «de las Cadenas», (Chains), Between the two doors the nave, which crosses the main one, stretches, forming a cross with it, symbol of Jesus Christ, and basic shape adopted by many Christian architects in the design of the temple plants through history.

La Costa del Sol

Mijas

The sixth chapel is that of, «La Virgen de los Reyes», (Our Lady of the Kings), because of a small wood carving over the left altar, which was for many years the companion of the Queen Isabel la Católica, in her innumerab'e journeys caused by military expeditions. After the reco quest of Málaga, the Catholic Kings donated it to the city. On both sides of the altar there are two wooden carvings, which represent Don Fernando, and Doña Isabel kneeling down, a work by Pedro de Mena. There exists also in this chapel a painting signed by Simonet, done at the end of the 19th century. One is filled with horror at its great fidelity, and accuracy. It represents the beheading of St. Paul.'

The ninth is in the centre of the «girola», and is called, of the Incarnation. It was designed by Villanueva in the neo-classic style: the French style subject to rigid rules, but of indisputable beauty. The copper and the silver combined with the marble and jasper to covey a sensation of perfect harmony.

The chapel of the Christ of the Amparo, (Refuge), is the eleventh. and is presided over by this wooden statue.

Number twelve is dedicatd to St. Julian, with a magnificent picture of, «El convite del fariseo», (the feast of the pharisee»), by Manrique, (Dutch school). This chapel leads to the Sacristy, (number thirteen), where a collection of paintings is shown.

The space where number fourteen should be is occupied by the Chains Door, mentioned before.

The seventeenth is the chapel of «La Buena Muerte», (the Good Death). It has two small carvings by Pedro de Mena. This Christ is the patron of the Spanish Army's first shock forces: The «Legion».

The last chapel, and number eighteen, is of St. Sebastián. It also has a Pedro de Mena crucified Christ.

EL ALTAR MAYOR (the High Altar).

On it we can see a Frapoli neo-classic tabernacle, with sculptures of saints and biblical personages. The paintings of the Passion that encircles the head are by Cesar de Arlasa.

The 18th. century organs are of Neoclassic style, but with certain Baroque elements. De la Orden endowed them with just under five thousand pipes. The sound is stereophonic, which combined with the so called «Cathedral effect», typical of these temples, create some acoustic effects of the best appreciated in music.

The pulpits are in marble by Aguirre, famous for his sculptures on the south façade of Charles V's Palace in Granada.

GIBRALFARO

Originally it must have been a Phoenician light house. The Moslems transformed it into military building. Yusuf I, Nazarite king, a great builder, reinforced the walls and modernised the structure turning it into a powerful fortress. Later on, when besieged several times, it was clear that the planning had been excellent, considering the times. Nevertheless, the great miltiary strength of the Christian armies, succeeded in overcoming it, but only after long and fierce fighting.

LA ALCAZABA

In Arabic it means fortress and was built in the 11th century, when the Granada kings annexed Málaga, over the remains of previous citadels. In the 14th century the bastions, walls and battlements were reinforced.

The Alcazaba was a citadel but in parts was also a residence. A combination of palatial refinement, taste and military structures very much to the taste of the Nazarites.

After the reconquest of Málaga by the Christians, since it served to no military purpose, it was gradually forgotten, up to the point of becoming a refuge for the most under-privileged people.

In the present times it treasures a very interesting Ar-chaeological museum with abundant pieces of the Egyp-tian, Greek, Carthaginian and Roman periods. It, also, con-tains a very interesting collection of ceramics from the se-veral stages of Moslem rule.

THE COSTA DEL SOL MALAGUEÑA

From Málaga going westwards and as far as St. Pedro de Alcántara, the international tourist zone most visited is located. Thousands of hotels of all types, shops which sell every imaginable thing... and more, luxury coaches, tourist groups, bustle. To hear people talk in so many foreign lan-guages surprises nobody. All the visitors are on holiday and, specially in summer, the place becomes an authenti-cal and amusing Babel, where some shops announce with humour that «Spanish is spoken».

Travelling in this direction we come across the Airport, the old military base of «El Rompedizo». It has magnificent runways and is very well fitted , with an air summer traffic, superior to most European airports.

Torremolinos is a bustling and lively town with a busy

Marbella

night life. The small and picturesque Torremolinos of the fifties, unfortunately, does not at all resemble the present town.

Fuengirola, twelve kilometres further to the west, has changed from an idyllic fishing village to a conglomerate of sky scrapers, plentiful shops, restaurantes and bars of all sorts.

It has seven kilometres of lovely beaches and a beautiful Sea Promenade «Paseo Marítimo» with sky scrapers towering high over it in some places. Thousands of people sunbathe on these beaches throughout the year; mainly visitors from all over the world.

MIJAS

Of very ancient origins, it is perched on the side of a 400 ms. high mountain. Later on, it became a very important Moslem military stronghold, since the Mijas fortress dominated the valley.

It resisted several sieges by the Christian armies. The

Marbella

Puerto Banús

chronicles narrate that in some of them even ladders were used. It fell, finally, in 1487. The inhabitants were made slaves and the citadel dismantled by an enraged Fernando de Aragón.

With the passing of time the special location and the whiteness of this typical Andalusian village, has charmed a large number of people. Today Mijas is an important commercial centre, where practically in every house there is a shop or a bar. On show there are a great variety of articles from typical local objects to jewellery, leather wear, and ceramics.

A donkey ride is an amusing and cheap pastime, very popular with the young.

The hermitage of Our Lady of the Peña, (Rock), a shrine very venerated in the town, was hewn in the rock by a friar between 1657 and 1682. It is believed to be very miracu-lous; the walls are covered with small votive offererings: parts of the body, arms, legs etc., placed there by grateful benefactors of the miracles, or favours.

MARBELLA

A few miles further, one arrives at Marbella, considered by many as the centre of the jet society, of the millionai-res, and great five star hotels.

If you are looking for an expensive present, you'll pro-bably find it in Marbella. Expensive true, but you'll have the statisfaction of spending your surplus money in five fo-reign languages.

Puerto Banús at the 171 km. with splendid restaurants, deserves a visit to admire the yachts, —some of them aut-hentic sailing jewels— breath the atmosphere, and maybe

Casares

Tajo de Ronda

squander some of your money eating in one of the restaurants.

A few kilometers further is San Pedro de Alcántara, where if your Rolls Royce breaks down, they will promptly fix it. This is not a joke. At San Pedro de Alcántara is the deviation to Ronda along the new road. This road is in good condition, very pcituresque, with beautiful views, on clear days of the African coast, and the Rock of Gibraltar. It is almost entirely new, and substitutes the dangerous and twisty old one. On the new road, by tourist coach, or car, one can get from San Pedro de Alcántara to Ronda in under one hour without going too fast.

RONDA

Not far from the existing Ronda, there was once an old town called Acinipo, which nine centuries B.C. was much visited by Phoenician merchants, who found, possibly, there and ideal place for their transactions.

It is today called, «Ronda la Vieja», (Old). Among the ruins part of an old theatre can be seen. The present Ronda, a few kilometers away from the other, «Arrunda» in Celtiberian times, was called Runda by the Greeks, and Munda by the Romans.

During the period 711-1485, Ronda was an important military centre called, «Medina al Runda». Because of its privileged location, it resisted furious Christian attacks on several occasions and a series of fictitious military manoeuvres were needed to deceive the brave Hamet el Zagri as well as almost 40.000 Christian soldiers and artillery to subdue it in 1485.

Due to its wildness and difficult territory, the surrounding mountains were, for a long time, centre of outlaws' activities. The majority of them rebels against the injusti-

ces and mediocrity of the people in office. In spite of their condition of outlaws they did not hesitate to fight loyally on the side of the King's army, to expel the Napoleonic troops during the War of Independence, 1808-1812.

Today Ronda is a town of more than 30.000 inhabitants. They are hospitable and kind people. It is the commercial centre of a zone mainly agricultural; a town of marked historic flavour, full of houses and palaces, which bear over their lintels, the many coats of arms of the noblemen who lived there once.

A visit to Ronda will not disappoint anybody.

The most noteworthy feature of Ronda is the great gorge. The locals call it, «el Tajo»; it really is a colossal precipice, 300 m. deep in places. A stone bridge, with three arches, called, «Puente Nuevo», (new bridge), has wrought iron railings, and joins the two parts of the town; the old or «ciudad», and the newer, dating back the reconquest 1485. From the new bridge the old Moorish one can be seen. There is an even older bridge, probably Roman: «El Puente de San Miguel».

Santa María la Mayor is a Christian 18th century church, built over a Moslem mosque. The styles are varied. The tower of «Mudejar», (Gothic-Morish) style, is Renais-

sance in its upper part. The facade balcony is 17th century.

After entering the temple, in a small room, remains of stucco work can be admired, with faded Arabic inscriptions of the old Mosque.

Further inside we find two architectonic styles: Gothic first, and 17th century Renaissance at the end of the church. There is a Baroque altar, 18th century, and on the left a La Roldand «Dolorosa», (Our Lady of Sorrows). The choir, in cedar and walnut wood, cuts the view of the nave. Although of anonymous author the carving of Biblical personages is excellent.

The High Altar, end of 18th century, is highly interesting and original, since it was done in pine wood. The author is also anonymous.

Walking along the medieval streets, a great many interesting houses and palaces are found, but we cannot enumerate them all in this brief work. Worthy of special mention: The Palace of Mondragón of Moslem origin, with mudéjar towers and a Renaissance entrance. It has been the residence of Princes and Kings several times.

La casa de Moctezuma which was built by the grandson of the famous Aztec King.

La casa del Rey Moro (House of the Moorish King) with 367 steps down to the river below.

La Plaza de Toros (Bull ring) is the oldest in the country (1748). Also one of the wider ones: 66 m in diameter.

On its facade we observe a wrought iron balcony with rich decorations of bulls.

The memory of the great master of bullfighting seems to float over this ring like a ghost among the old columns. Pedro Romero, member of an old bullfighting family of old lineage, founder of the famous Escuela de Ronda (Ronda bullfighting School). It is said of him that he killed more than 6.000 bulls without suffering any injury.

In this bullring every year a «Corrida» called Goyesca takes place, where all dress in the Goya times fashion. If anyone feels like seeing it, it is necessary to book for a place several months ahead.

ARTURO PORCEL MORCILLO

Translation:
M.J. López
T.D. Dobson

Cueva de Nerja

Nerja (Cuevas)

Tolox

Y vos viajero, ¿Dónde vais?
A Granada que es mi patria
¡Y buena patria a fe mía!
replicó don Quijote.
(Cervantes)

Campana la de la Vela
La del dorado plañir
que en la noche nos despierta
para besarnos y huir

GRANADA

Reclining of the furthest foothills of the Sierra Nevada and with the green carpet of the valley extended at its feet is the city of Granada, once the capital of the Nazirite kingdom in the era of Muslim Spain. It sprawls over three main hillsides, those of the Albaicín, the Alhambra, and the Mauror, corresponding to the three main communities of Granadian middle ages, the muslim community, the sultans'home, and the jewish quarter.

Today, the city slopes gently down to the fertile plain of farmland. The harvests of both the northern and southern parts of this flatland have been admired since ancient time.

The province of Granada covers a surface of 12.531 km., giving an extrenely irregular contour to the land, reaching from the highest altitude in Spain the 3.481 meters of Peak Mulhacén, descending on the eastern side to the meditterranean.

Due to this irregular geography, there are distinct tracts of land between the mountains and the sea. Among them is the Alpujarra. It lies in the north, like an intermediary between mountain peaks and the plain, a green lake stretching to the Lecrín valley. This provincial capital sits 680 metres above sea level, making it one of the highest capitals in Spain. Its climate is continental and its population is something near 300.000 inhabitants.

Its history is well-known, proved by the many archeological sites. They contain a million witnesses to the history of the city, in the coins minted in the fith century in the name of Iliberis, and the remains of Phoenician, Greek, Carthigan, and Roman civilizations. Newer remains like these, are found especially along the coasts, the traces of the Visigoths, who opened up the way for the muslims who, in their turn, left the most beatiful evidence of Arab dominion in the whole peninsula - that of the Alhambra and the Generalife, whose fame strechtes across the world.

19

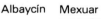

THE ALHAMBRA

They surround the three patios, architectural models of Arab-Andalusia inherited from the design of mediterranean houses with the functional and practical taste of Arab-Andalusians.

The first room we enter is called the "MEXUAR", the hall of justice. It has four columns in the centre that show the original design. Later on in the Christian times it was turned into a chapel. The other attractions here are the veranda with drawings of Pompei, the little basin for holy water, and some coats of arms of Charles V with the "Plus-Ultra" motto.

In some of the inscriptions of the hall we can see Arabic letters which say "If you ask for justice, it will be given to you". This made people think it was the Hall of Justice. However, the Old Palace is full of phrases from the Quran, moral aphorisms and praises to Allah. It isn't believed, however, that the Alhambra was a place of prayer.

Near the base we can see some windows of what was once a pulpit or lecturn or perhaps a place of meditation with a niche or mihrab turned to the rising sun. It reads "Don't dally, como to prayer".

The view dominating this lecturn will be with you for the whole visit even in the Generalife. It is the Albaicin, the old Granada, the Arab Granada, full of carmens (private gardens), the typical houses of Granada, old churches, all of which are ancient mosques, narrow streets as they were in the middle ages, and the caves of Sacromonte— the gypsy quarter, capped by the old medieval protecting wall of Granada.

Adjacent to this there is a square patio with a room on the north side called "the Golden Room" and opposite is one of the most beautiful facades of this palace, finished with a bold and noble cornice— one of the best examples of Granadian-Arab carpentry anywhere— in a facade which commemorates the conquest of Algecires. In the centre of the patio is a fountain with a wide marble bowl. It is a copy of the original which was moved in the time of Charles V.

Through the passageway past a sharp corner we come to a big rectangular courtyard with a large pool in the centre. On either side of it are rows of myrtle bushes. At the northern and southern ends are elegant arched porticoes supported by beautifully carved columns. This must have been the public and official part of the palaces, but there are resting places for beds or sofas here, too. The pool reflects like a mirror the northern and southern facades. It also refreshes the air on hot summer days. It used to soothe the dusty traveller, enabling him to continue his way refreshed. The angles of this courtyard are placed so as to provide shade in the summer and sun in the winter.

Behind the southern gallery the solid stone structure of the palace of Charles V looms up as if desiring to enter this very courtyard.

20

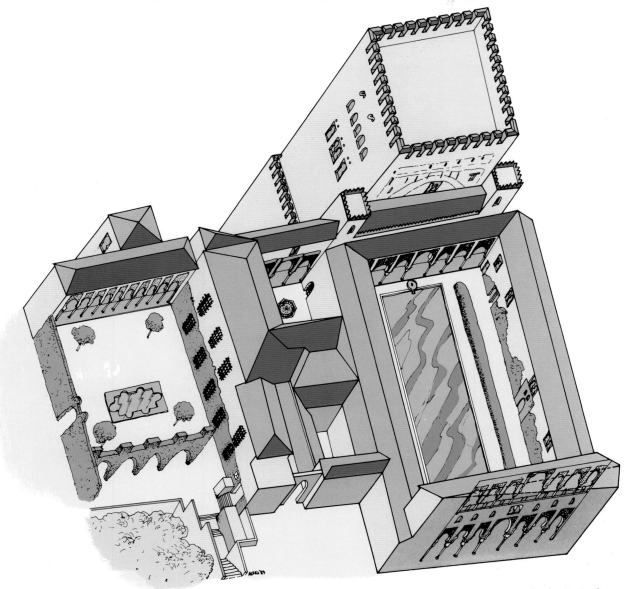

On the other side is the COMARES TOWER and the THRONE ROOM OR THE AMBASSADORS ROOM, as it is also called. You can see niches at each step of the entrances that were used as places to put perfume or incense.

In this tower of the Throne Room is a big wooden dome where the colours have faded. It used to represent the heaven of the Muslims. There are more than 8.000 pieces of inlaid wood in it. The large windows open eastward, westward, and northward. This augments the inner view of the Alhambra and it would not be the same at all without them. Ceramic panelling surrounds the base of the rooms and the walls of the open places. All of the rooms are covered in stucco and carved or moulded clay, where we can still make a good guess as to the original colours that were there. The Alhambra was painted in reds, blues, greens, and golds. The phrases here on the walls, show us without doubt that this was the place where the ambassadors were recieved and where the sultan presided and where everyone had to show the greatest respect. This is where the biggest decisions in the sultanate of Granada were taken. The sultanate contained then, a much larger geographical area than the Andalusia of today.

In the centre room of the northern section is an inscription which says "I am as the heart is to the body". In other words, the most important position is that of the sultan. All the windows here had coloured glass which gave the room an air of mystery and respect. Even at the base-level, it was possible to open little windows and take a look at the view.

In the centre, we can see some mudejares mosaics. (Mudejares is the name of the special art of the Granadian-Arab after the first conquest of the city. Some of the original work is in the Archeological Museum). This work is proof of the quality of the mudejares ceramics.

Through this little, seemingly insignificant, more ignored and almost secret door is the harem. The world knows it as the COURTYARD OF THE LIONS.

Our friend, dear Visitor, if this is your first time here, you may feel a little decieved because of the photographs, engravings and films, which, with their technology, have perhaps shown something more grandiose, sensational, or monumental. The reality is the opposite. It is secluded, well-porportioned, and intimate. These qualities the Arabs passed to us as a refuge from ostentaciousness. Such a contrast from renaissance and gothic styles it is! Only a short time should be needed to appreciate its porportions in balance— nothing too big or too small and all functional and exquisite from every angle. This is the harem. That word does not mean, as we have been led to believe, a place of a lot of women. No, It means the special annexes for the intimate family.

The rectangular "marjal" surface area, (an Arab agrarian measure of 528 square metres) with two pavillions, one on each side, is garlanded with columned galleries — 124 columns in all-all done in Almerian marble of Macael. The surround the famous fountain of twelve lions, an heretical sculpture with an oriental bowl which spews out water from the mouths of the lions after is gushes from a central jet. At the edge of the fountain is carved one of the most beautiful poems of the Alhambra. It is an eulogy of thes mansions and gardens and the sultan which, like the fountain, showers honour and force on its soldiers - the lions of war.

Historians and scholars assure us that the squares between the water channels, now full of stones of Mengibar, were once gardens, perhaps lower than they are now, in which case the scene would have appeared like a tapestry and the shrubs and flowers would have covered the plinths, bases of

22

Sala de las Dos Hermanas

ALHAMBRA &

1.- ALCAZABA
2.- P. CARLOS V
3.- P. JUSTICIA
4.- PILAR CARLOS V
5.- F. MEXUAR
6.- T COMARES
7.- LINDARAJA
8.- LEONES
9.- PARTAL & T. DAMAS
10.- JARDINES BAJOS
11.- PATIO ACEQUIA
12.- PATIO SULTANA

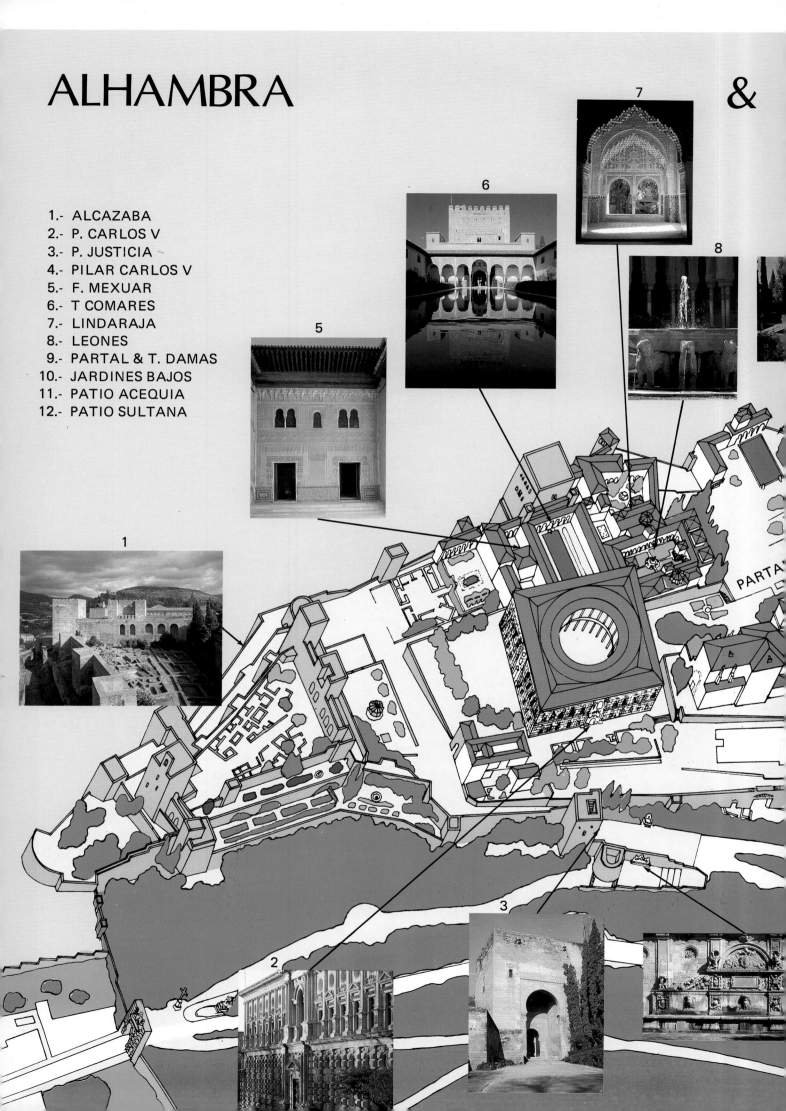

PARTA

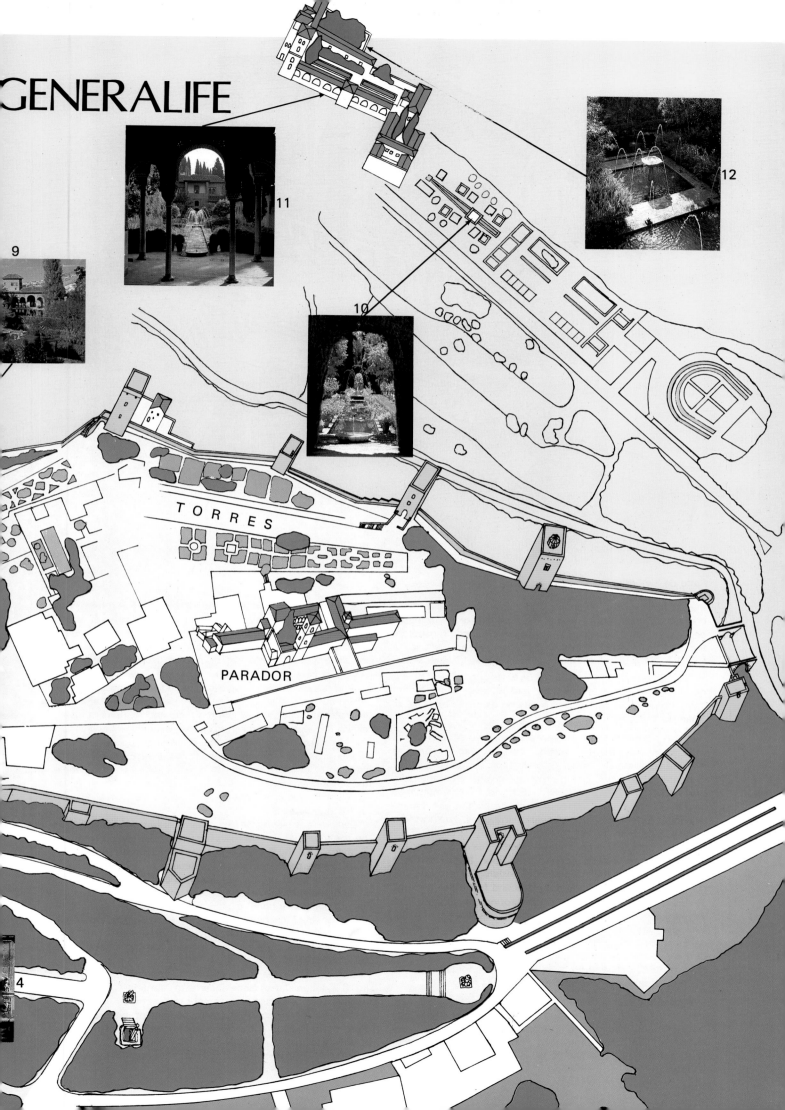

GENERALIFE

9

11

10

12

TORRES

PARADOR

4

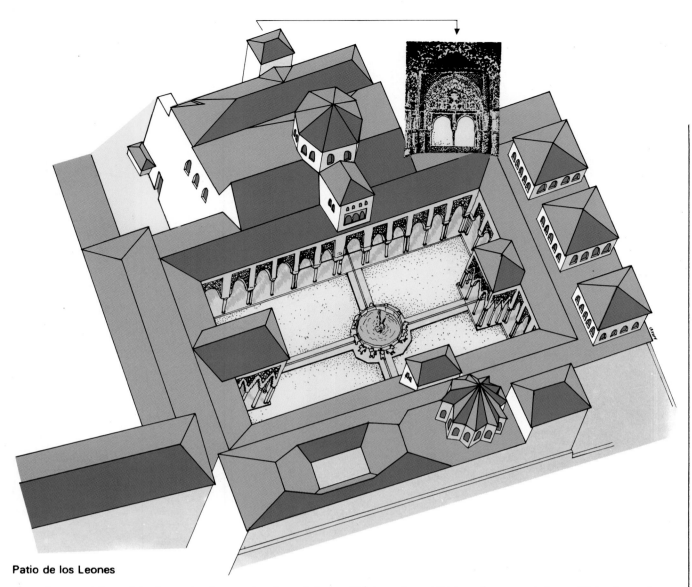

Patio de los Leones

the columns, giving originality and colour to the view of the courtyard. From another angle, the scene looks like an oasis, or a forest of palm trees with the sky lit and transparent through its interlacing branches. Some might even say it looks like a Christian cloister as seen through an Islamic mind.

There is one thing that assures us of its originality. There is no single precedent of this courtyard in either Morroco nor any Oriental country. It is a unique and exquisite example of Spanish-Arabian art.

In the northern and southern side are two square rooms with beautiful molded plaster covering an interesting mocarabes dome decorated with stalactites which are easier to contemplate when laying down on divans. The southern room is called the ''ABENCERRAJES'', and it has memories of the killings of the nobles of Granada by the last sultan, Boabdil, probably because of political intrigues. The northern room is popularly called the room of the TWO SISTERS because of the two large stones of marble (as all of them, the work of Maceal) which are set in the floor. In one of these rooms we can see the inscription. Translated, it means, ''The stars of Heaven would gratefully descend from their celestial vault to this smaller vault to rotate around the sultan''. This would seem to indicate that this room was reserved for the exclusive use of the sultan or king. In this room, as in the Abencerrajes, appear two shelves or bed places and from one of them descended a staircase which was removed during the time of the Christian reforms. It was possible to descend into the turkish baths or ''hammam'' by this stairway.

Behind the pavillion of the courtyard are two rooms. One has a ceiling of half-Christian design with a base of the original Arabic. The door on the side was perhaps the original entrance. The room opposite is called the ''Kings''. It has been the subjetc of debate because in the ceiling of three of its intimate little rooms there are paintings of human beings.

The koranic prohibition of representations of living forms has caused many people to believe this was Christian work. However, the latest theory is that this is the work of Arabs in Arab times but that it shows a relaxation of the strict religious injunctions during the last and most decadent period of Arabic culture in the Spanish penninsula.

And now, our friend, traveller, we can reflect on its history. The courtyard was built in 1374 under the sultanate of Muhammad V, during which the taste and refinements were clear. The water was taken from many kilometers away from the river Darro and was deposited in large pools built at a higher level than these palaces. It ran down to lower levels, causing all of the fountains to sing - a luxury for the people from hot countries.

Water flowed everywhere by system unknown in all Europe of the middle ages.

Earlier we spoke of the ''hammam'' or bath which was built on the tower level. The Arab hammam was copied from the Romans. Like the Roman one, it was divided into three parts-apotiterium, caldaerium, and tepiderium, or in other words, a steam room, for producing sweat, a cold bath room and a resting room for when the bath is finished. Without going into unnecessary detail explanation, we can say that this is the method of cleaning the body by persperation, or, as we know it, a sauna. The resting room of the bath has two lounging rooms which seem to indicate the importance of the relaxation period after the bath. The decor, as some experts seem to think, is the result of a badly done restoration dome in 1844 when Queen Isabel II came to Granada. Colours were used which could hint at the colour in the stucco-work of the rest of the Alhambra. The upper balconies of this room were used by musicians and singers for the entertainment of the sultan and his family. Popular fantasies insist that the musicians were álways blind so that they were unable to gaze on the family of the sultan at their bath.

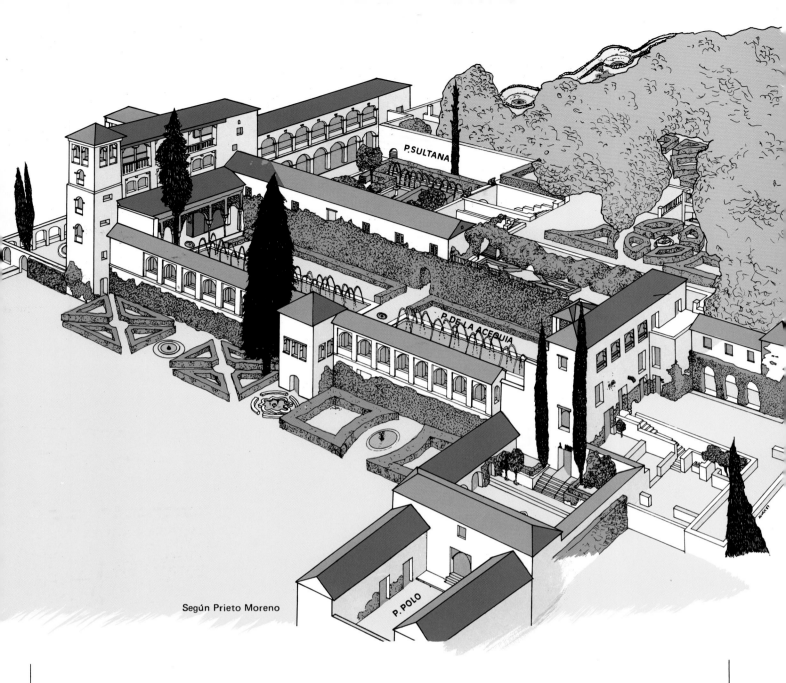

Según Prieto Moreno

THE GENERALIFE

Very close to the Alhambra and almost joined, but only by a banonet-like pathway between two walls, is the Generalife. It is possible to walk from the Nazarite palaces to this great garden, the place of pleasure and recreation of the Granadian sultans. It adorns one of the most beautiful positions found in Granada.

It is a private garden, and like an anonymous romantic said, "A garden beyond compare". It wasn't garden of western design. The garden for the Arab-Andalusian was mixture of "apparent disorder in order", a mixture of flowers, fruits and other domestic plants with many perenials (myrtle and bay), pools, and flowing channels of water to both irrigate and delight. Some of it is sowed with greens, aubergines, or artichokes and trimmed with a border of lilies or spikenard plants. It is composed of a contrast of colours and smells camoflauged by lemon and orange trees or other fruit trees dispersed according to the taste of the gardener. Such a combination of delights we could never initate even in our best-planned perennial gardens.

The residence is in the uppermost part of the layout. A channel of silently and constantly flowing water crosses a very beautiful courtyard garden between two arched galleries. The harmony and beauty are predominant in the whole scene which is completed with a unique view over the towers and

and peaceful countryside and also stretches to the theatrical view of the tiny streets and towers of the antique Granadian town-the Albaycín.

What is now called the Generalife, the paradise of the sultans, the Generalife seen by visitors is onty a small part of what it once was. When this heritage was passed on by its last owner, the Spanish count of Campotejar to the Spanish state, it was verified that it had been much more enormous when it came under the governance of the Catholic Monarchs after the conquest of the city. It was used farmland and grazing for livestock. The fertile domestic gardens that are known and open to the public and can be visited while touring the Alhambra, have, with the passing of time, been transformed back into gardens. Their characteristics, though quite different than they were in muslim times, are still beautiful and give the viewer a somewhat more western view of a garden.

The water taken from the Darro river, by an enormous and ingenious work of the fourteenth century, runs through a part of the Valparaíso valley and into a large reservoir situated in the upper part of the building. It spawns the various sensual sounds that are made by falling water, both seen and unseen, from the sequencial platforms needed because the estate is situated on the south west side of the so-called "Hill of the Sun".

31

Patio de la Acequia

Jardín Bajo del Generalife

THE PALACE OF CHARLES V

If there is one monument that is polemical, misunderstood and yet indispensably quoted as excepcional, it is the Palace of Charles V. A series of old prejudices and a thorough ignorance of the role played by Granada in the projects of the 16th century Spanish monarchy have been decisive factors.

We could say that people still believe in the romantic clichés, so dear to 19th century travellers, of a Moslem world destroyed by the incomprehension of a few fierce Spanish monarchs who want to make a clean sweep of everything. The real history is quite different. Nowadays any historian knows the symbolic value that the Spanish monarchy gave to the conquest of Granada. As such a symbol, the recently conquered city will become the point of convergence of the most varied artist, Spaniards as well as Italians, who will have to give it the magnificience of a Christian capital; the same that it had in the Moslem period. Therefore, there existed a "political intention" of strengthening with grand royal constructions, the sense of "capitality" that it had enjoyed for centuries.

If we take into that the Catholic Monarchs had already erected a Funeral Chapel here, we will be able to understand why their grandchil, the Emperor, identified himself with the project and, as is logical in one who ruled the destinies of Europe, was concerned about developing it.

The occasion was unique: during his honeymoon with the Empress Isabel in 1526, the Emperor visited the Alhambra and lodged in the rooms that, from then onwards, would be known as "the lodgings of Charles V". There he establishes his appreciation for the ancient Nasrite precinct and his admiration will lead him to wish to enhance and enlarge it, making it suitable for the needs of a modern Court.

The outcome of all this, is the assignment of the Palace of Charles V to the man who was in position of trust, the Marquis of Mondéjar, governor of the Alhambra.

This personage, fundamental for the history of the Palace, belongs to one of the great families of the Spanish nobility, the Mendoza, who from Toledo had contributed to spreading, throughout Spain, a liking for the new Renaissance art, thanks to his Italian upbringing. One must remember that, th, through the great warriors, ambassadors or princes of the Church, these families of the nobility were the first to came into contact with the great revolution that took place in Italy in the artistic field that we call even in the entrance to the Nasrite precinct with the fountain of Charles V, designed by Pedro de Machuca, the same designer of the palace where the coat of arms of Tendilla, the one of the city and of the Empire coexist and cohabit with the ornamental repertory of the finest classicism and that was elaborated in 1543 by Niccolao da Corte.

The Emperor, contrary to what his son Philip II will do in the future, had no specific interest in the carrying out of his works; he gave general instructions and delegated their execution to specific people in a position of trust, which is the reason why one cannot speak of a "Charles V style" all over the Empire.

But together with the desire to highlight Granada as the new capital of Christianity, we must take into account a more generalized phenomenon that will give rise to what G. Kubler calls "the Italianized South", referring to Andalusia as a place outside Italy where the ideas of Renaissance were best received.

That is due to a double polarity: Seville, centre of trade with the West Indies and Granada as the symbolic capital of a century-long fight against the Islamic world. The final result is the Palace of Charles V is not an isolated fact, but another link in that desire to join the modern throbbing of life which is taking hold of the whole of Andalusia.

It is necessary to remember that Pedro Mártir de Anglería, an Italian in Tendilla's court and Juan Boscán, the introducer of the new Renaissance poetry talked about the new poetry in these gardens.

Within the generalized atmosphere of admiring the style called "Roman" as the best, is where we will be able to understand not only the work of the Palace of Charles V, but also the outstanding works of his Secretary, D. Francisco de los Cobos, in Ubeda or in Baeza.

But, what is, in fact, the meaning of the Palace?

Professor Cepeda defined it, accurately, as the symbol of a reign that began with great impetus and that never was finished off; the covering of the second storey, let's remember, is a modern work.

The financing of the work was the responsability of the Moriscos, and this circumstances created two problems: in the first place, the Moriscos had to hand over their income which, according to the most learned officials, had previously been assigned to hospitals and to care, thus resulting quite incongrous that the Christian King should use it for his house; secondly, the revolt of the Moriscos, one of the harshest civil wars, destroyed the kingdom of Granada, we would say that forever, which would prevent the complete development of the initial proyect.

Pedro Machuca who will be in charge of the works, had a sound Italian education due to having worked in Rome with Michelangelo and with Raphael. But moreover, thanks to that training, he was able to know the most elaborate creations of the Renaissance in their theoretic aspects. The proof of it is the choice of a very singular ground plan, of a circular court within a square which represents the most profound aspirations of the ideal design since the days of Alberti.

We can trace the precedents from "Saint Peter's in Montoro in Rome, that must have been surrounded by a circular court according to the plan published by Serlio, to the circular court of the "Villa Madama" by Raphael or the drawings of palaces by Leonardo da Vinci.

The original design, today in the Library of the Royal Palace of Madrid, proposed that there should be in front of each of the south and west façades respectively, squares with arcades but these were never executed. The interior, with the court that has thirty metres of light, and has forty-two metres of diameter, is organized with large lateral halls, except for the NW cant in which the Capel and the Crypt are situated.

The latter was, in fact, the room that Charles V paid most attention to, since on the 30th November 1527, on receiving the project, he wrote: "I only want to tell you that the front room must be large and that inside it there should be a Chapel to say and hear Mass". But in that original plan one could already see the new Royal House as a theatrical enlargement of the old rooms of the Nasrite enclosure.

Machuca was in charge of the works until his death in 1550; his son Luis succeeded him and, later, Juan de Orea who had to be subject to the instructions given to him by Juan de Herrera in what concerned the staircases and the upper part of the main façade, and Minjares had to finish that stage.

The interior is characterized by a complete sobriety and bareness: two storeys with lintels of a Doric and Tuscan order and a large main staircase which links up with the magnificent annular barrel vault of the foyer. All of this being done with that wisdom so characteristic of Machuca, as regards the stereotomy which made a wonder of precision out of every block of cut stone.

The façade is carried out having as a base a continuous stone bench (springer) over which two storeys rise up, the first with a rustic bossage, of a deep-rooted Italian tradition emphasizes the horizontaly of the whole, and the second with Ionic pilasters on a pedestal where different embossing is carried out, one notes a tense contrast of lightness and verticaly. The windows blend the rectangular design with the

Carlos V. Fachada

35

circular openings on both storey, thus restoring the linear play dominant in Renaissance style.

The scuptural decoration offers special interest, as it is executed according to a refined humanistic programme of symbols and allegories that, logically, centre on the figure of the Emperor as Caesar. Mythology allows a comparison between Charles V and Heracles (Hércules) in the embossing of the main façade or the simple recollection of the battle of Pavía, are the femenine personages on the South façade.

All these sculptures the work, in addition to the aforementioned artist, of Juan de Orea and Antonio de Leval, make up the specific visualization of an imperial message which clearly shows itself from the till of the Alhambra to the conquered city.

The palace is erected over a Christian quarter, a subsequent annex to the Nasrite enclosure. A geometric error caused its creation to affect in a minimum way, the scheme of the enclosure of the Alhambra, in which case, and in no other,

one has to understand the reasons for such a radical and new projects as was the Palace of Charles V.

Probably thanks to the Palace, the Alhambra became part of the patrimony of the Royal Palaces of Spain instead of being limited to representing an archeological testimony of a defeated culture.

CONCEPCION FELEZ LUBELZA
Professor of History of Art.
University of Granada.

La Catedral

Capilla Real. Reja. ➡

CHRISTIAN GRANADA

In 1453, the Turks took Constantinople and the Ottoman and so threatened the Christian world. During that time, the Catholic Monarchs, after imposing relative peace in the Christian kingdoms, defeated the muslims in the kingdom of Granada, the last stronghold of Islamic political power in Europe. This meant a triumph of the cross over the half-moon, and all of Christianity celebrated this great victory. Granada, then, became the symbol of the Christian victory over the muslims and so compensated for the loss of Constantinople.

The Catholic Monarchs, before the conquest, had chosen Toledo as their burial place, but now has decided to be buried in Granada, accentuating thus the historical importance of the events of the victory. The last wishes of the Queen made it clear. She indicated her desire to be laid to rest in the city of Granada. A royal order of September 13, 1504, decreed that a chapel should be built next to the cathedral and named as the "Royal Chapel" under the spiritual protection of the saints John the Baptist and John the Evangelist.

The work was rapidly done and in 1521, it was practically finished. It was done in the decadent gothic or so-called Isabeline-gothic style. The design was entrusted to Enrique de Egas, from Burgos.

The chapel presents only one exterior façade because it is joined to the cathedral on the other side, the "Church of the Sagrario", and it is joined to the old exchange market on the other.

The temple inside depicts a plant with a latin cross 50.80 metres long and 21.80 metres wide. The church is practically divided into two parts by a large grille done in the plateresque style sculpted in metal by Bartolomé de Jaén. Scenes of the Passion are in the upper part, the apostles are depicted on the columns and the emblen of Ferdinand and Isabel is in the centre.

Behind the grille, there are two sepulchres of Italian marble from Carrara. The figures of Ferdinand and Isabel are on the right. These were carved by the Italian, Alexandro Domenico Fanccelli. On the left, raised a little higher, and done in a more ostentatious sytle, are the figures of Juana the Mad and Phillipe the Handsome, sculpted by Bartolomé Ordóñez. Under the sepulchres is a crypt with five coffins of lead enclosed by bronze bands. The central ones contain the remains of Ferdinand and Isabel. The ones on the side, those of Juana and Phillipe and the small one contains the remains of Prince Micheal, a grandson of the Catholic Monarchs.

CAPILLA REAL

Bartolomé de Jaen

Bartolomé Ordoñez

Mausoleos. D. Fernando y Doña Isabel

Domenico Fancelli

Sacristía
Capilla Real. Dierik Bouts

Catedral. Arco Toral
y Capilla Mayor

CATEDRAL

On the side of the transept, is found an extraordinary triptych of Dierik Bouts. The largest altar, of exceptional beauty, is made of gold-plated wood and polychrome. It has figures of St. John and the martyrs in scenes of the Passion and the Crucifixion, made in France by the little known French artist Felipe de Vigarny.

On the right of the transept, is the entrance to the museum, the treasury of this capital chapel and sacristy. The treasury is composed of some of the personal possesions of the Catholic Monarchs, bequeathed to the capel (a crown, a jeweled coffer, a sword, a prayer book, and some other things). Special mention should be given to collection of fifteenth century Flemish, Italian, and Spanish paintings also bequeathed by the Monarchs. It is one of the most significant collections of art now in Spain and contains some of the best works signed by such artists as Memling, Perugino, Dierik Bouts, Roger van der Weyden, Boticcelli, and Berruguete.

D. Siloe (Capilla Mayor)

Catedral Vidriera. Theodor van Holland

These heralded the end of the Arab-Muslim civilisation in Spain and brought to a close the era of gothic style which lasted somewhat longer in this country than elsewhere. This Cathedral is one of the last monuments built in this style.

THE CATEDRAL

The date of March 25, 1523, the day of the Incarnation (Easter), saw the first stone laid in one of Spain's most interesting monuments, though it is overshadowed by, an almost ingnored by the world of tourism, due to the greater fame of the Alhambra.

The work of designing it was originally entrusted to Enrique de Egas who also directed the construction of the Royal Chapel. The plan is similar to that of the cathedral in Toledo, in the same gothic style. On this foundation, Diego de Siloé took over the architectural direction using the structural base of the gothic and created on it the first renaissance cathedral in Spaing. This was the new style which immediately caused repercussions in Málaga, Jaén and Guadix.

Five names, or sections, run through the building from the entrance to the frontispice. They are supported by large pillars which culminate in an elegant vaulted ceiling. At the longest end, it is 115.40 metres by 67.25 metres and the largest dome reaches 45 metres in height.

The two greatest innovations of Siloé, called the "siloescan solution", and which created a new school of art, are

a) the superimposition of levels and styles to achieve greater height and luminosity without breaking the overall proportion, and

b) the juxtaposition of the triumphal arches which are used at once to complete the principal section and to support the perfectly circular vaulted dome with the arches reaching up to a single point.

Many valuable altars, retables, paintings and sculptures adorn all sides of the cathedral, and were designed in the original architectural plan. The choir was designed to surround the altarpiece in order to permit maximum visibility from the entrance at the far end of the building. So, the choir setting does not obscure the artworks as it does in most other cathedrals. Two inmense baroque organs dating from 1748, raise their golden trumpets on the sides of the central nave, drawing the eye to the main altar, the upper part of which opens to a spendid set of stained glass windows produced in Flander in the time of Charles the V.

Below the stained glass and surrounding the main altar, one can see an excellent collection of paintings done by Alonso Cano, who was born in Granada in 1601 —a painter, sculptor and architect. The paintings represent scenes of the life of the Virgen. Central to this group of windows, paintings and sculpture of the altar is a great tabernacle of silver supported by a base of serpentine stone.

There was an attempt to decorate many more places of the church with this gold plating, but because of the cost, it was limited to the main altar, thougt it illuminates and brings out the brillance of the altar, contrasting it to the white of the walls making one of the most original and surprising views a religious building can give.

44

Claustro

San Jerónimo

CARTUJA

When Granada was no larger than its old city-walls, what its perimeters did not overflow into the concrete urban districts we seem to much to prefer nowadays, the life of the city was slow. Animal power was the principal source of transport and the city did not suffer from pollution as it does now. So, the site of the Cartusian Monastery originally was in an idyllic and tranquil spot, excellent for meditation, spiritual vigils and retreats.

After much turmoil and discussion between don Gonzalo Fernández, the original sponsor, and the monks, the construction finally began in 1517. Many delays later, due to economic problems and the dependency of its direction of the head of the Order, it was finished. A most spectacular sacristy and "Holy of Holies" are part of it. The work was entrused to Francisco Hurtado Izquierdo who told the monks that all he designed in the architectural plan was shaped into the decor.

The monastery actually consists of a beautiful cloister around which are the monks dining room, another room and two chapels. The church is of only one nave, separated into parts for the separate places to be used by the lay faithful, the novices, and the superiors, by means of grilles, doors and panes of glass. A stone battlement runs through the main part of the nave to what, in theory, could be the transept, coming to the altar, where the gold-plated baroque work exemplifies and prepares us for the sight of the most distinguished art of this type that has been done in Spain.

A door on the left side, inlaid in precious jewels, introduces us to the sacristy. Our attention in monopolized by a world of very baroque white plaster stucco-work, contrasting with both the little-known marbles of Lanjarón and the chests meticulously made by the brother of the order, Friar Vázquez. Saint Bruno, the founder of the order, is shown on the main altar of this sacristy and on a small one on the left, an excellent work in polychrome wood by José de Mora. Crowning this annexe, necessary for a religious order as populous as this one was, is an eliptical dome painted by the brother in the order, Friar Tomás Ferrar. It is notably darker in colour than it was originally when it was concieved to highlight the light clear tones and luminosity of the art in the grouping.

Past the main altar, and separated by a panel of Venician glass, we find the "Holy of Holies", the sancta sanctorium, the placae where the holy sacrament was given. An intricate niche in marble by Cabra of Córdoba accomodates an insignificant shrine of olive and sandalwood, which substitute for the original of rock crystal, which disappeared, like so much art, during various invasions and historical upheavals. It is lit from the only window in this part, making it shine and sparkle. It can be seen in a straight line from the entrance of the church, and gives a sensational effect of celestial light for both the lay people and the clergy alike.

Four statues stand in the corners. They are of Mary Magdalena, Saint Bruno, Saint John, and Saint Joseph, work of Mora, Risueño, and Duke Cornejo. Threatening and serene at the same time, they guard the dome, done by Valazquez and the Cordoban Palomeno, perhaps one of the best works in silk, an imposing scale of leaf-work in arced, commanding and heavy frills in this baroque style.

Cartuja Sacristía

El mauror

GRANADA

The newer, Christian civilization has imposed itself since 1492. The Gothic styles lasted longer here, died here to be suceeded here as well, by the beauty and flowering of the Renaissance and the exuberant and multicoloured Baroque. All these make Granada one of the most interesting Spanish cities on any tourist itinerary. Complementing this wide artistic range are its beautiful wiews, and added attraction to this world famous city. From the Arab era, and with the lodging of the Chancellory here, Granada was, up until recently, a military city of importance, unparalleled in its layout in all of eastern Andalusia.

Because it sits next to the Sierra Nevada where the sun greets it first and bids farewell last, and it is removed from the busy crossroads of commerce, it has a feeling of being remote, unknown and mysterious.

The first time you come to Granada, you may come with a spirit predisposed towards the mysterious, the unexpected dream, perhaps a result of the tales of romantic visitors of the nineteenth century who believed that they had found an oriental city in the west. It appeared to them as a beautiful jeweled odalisque in the moon-lit night, projecting fantasies into a marvellous range of lengends, tales of captive princesses, hidden treasures, magicians, fortune tellers and epic tales which have, for many generations shaped the expectation of visitors, no matter where they come from or who they are.

Granada, after suffering the scourge of the debatable in quality, if not outright awful reconstruction work, still maintains the spirit of its special originality, grace and style which could hardly disappoint whoever visits it, though, a poet once commented on its fate thus, ''Granada of your power - nothing remains''. Still, it retains the flowering in its surface and texture the nobility, the refinement of beauty achieved in times long gone.

Sta. Ana

Chancillería

THE ALPUJARRA

istorians do not agree, neither ancient nor modern, about the meaning of the term "Alpujarra".

Aben Rashid called it the Land of the Sirgo, or silk, because of the great quantity produced in Arab times. Luis del Mármol translates the term as "the resentful" or "the untamed", a separated area in the time of the caliphate. The geographical dictionary of Madoc translates it the Al-Bordjela castile of the allies. It is said that Suar el Kaici and other rebels who put up forts in the mountains surrounding Granada, were named with this term. Sharif Al-Idriss called it Albugscharra, the Sierra of the pastures. Simonet deduced "Albuxarrat" from "Alba Sierra". It seems incongruous to have so many translations of only one term, one word. Whatever it means, it refers to a wide area on the south-east slopes of the Sierra Nevada. bordered on the west by the peak of the Veleta, on the lower slopes by the rivers of Lanjarón and Orgiva, and on the extreme east by the Sierra de Láujar, sloping to the Castell de Ferro. It comprises some eleven leagues, or about 55 km in lenght by about 35 km in width, extending from the Sierra Nevada to the sea.

It was a very turbulent area during the time of the Cordoban emirate because of its independence and concern for its own interests. It was not conquered by the Arabs until 711 after the battle of Guadalete. Even then, it retained special concessions and privileges of religion and other things.

The steepness of its terrain, its deep valleys, its cliffs and peaks made the Alpujarra practically inaccessable until modern times. Its silk market, and cultivation of the Mulberry tree and the raising of silk-worms during the middle ages for the silk of the Nazarite reign competed with the silks of the east.

It was a scene of bloody battles during the Arab revolts, especially during the time of Carlos V and Felipe II. It lost its greatness after the loss of the silk industry and became a place of raising livestock and cultivation of crops so difficult as to be an heroic effort. Today we can look back and admire the titanic effort sustained to eke out a precarious existence here. A saying of the province of Granada claims, "It is better to be a worker in the valley than a property owner in the Alpujarra". This indacates how difficult it was.

This is the Alpujarra, a wide region with forever sloping sides, a view never flat, always dramatic, reclining back on its slopes to breathe in the sky during the day and the stars at night.

Snow blankets it in winter, the ravines shade it in the summer. Here the poplar stand erect, the fig spills out its branches, the chestnut raises itself tall and grand, looking wild and unpruned, giving its ruby-like fruit or shedding its leaves as if doffing jewellry, sometimes late and sometimes early in the year. The corn lined up in rows appear like little armies made up of tufts of straw, bending in the breeze. The vines crouch low and mature into the ochre colour in the sun, eventually aging into raisins. The olive plays hide and seek between the green plants, its bark the grey colour of ash since forever and until forever. From luscious oak to luscious oak, the trees stretch out their arms as if calling to an absent friend or lifting their branches like the miller's hefty wife kneading out not bread, but the sun and the storms together, letting light and shade fall in fingers, hiding their fruit which is the food for small animals, squirrels, and swine. Little villages are sprinkled on the peaks and sides of the mountains like the dew-spots of lime on the rocks, born of the work of scrawny hands. Wealth and power seems filtered out, leaving only a

La Alpujarra

hard life of toil on the dreamy river-banks and the sea so near yet so far.

Tertiary waste land lies scorched of every summit and slope and flows into the gullies. The stones seem to know of the many waters past and present and wait paciently in the all-encompassing fog.

The various shores appear as if they are riding bleached pack-saddles of the rivers, both defining the tranquility and breaking the silence. It is quiet and dreamy. The sun rises over the grey rock terraces and the moon shines restlessly from time to time outlining the grey slate stones, which give shelter to sparrows and swallows.

The fountains, the eternal fountains pour out their many voices claiming an ancestral right to occupy the walls of the houses reminding us of the sound of litanies now and then sung by the choruses in churches. Then there is the tower, erect and straight, outlining the horizon. The weather vane turns its head defining the wind and visible at dawn which joins the plaza and the porches in one tone of colour.

On must feel the pain that was and is in the Alpujarra. It lasted so long and was so deep that it is embedded and part of it. Nodaways, one may still sense it in the future, as well as the past.

White lime has engraved vertical lines on the walls, adorning and making a contrast for the geraniums and roses with their perfume. The gravepines climb between the parts of the walls like candles looking for the heat and light of the humanity of the household, then extend their branches to cluster overhead shading the golden sun courting the mild autumn.

The woman of the village would sweep the door so much that the dust returned to turn her grey at the temples. She would spend her entire life in the backrooms of shops or rooms of houses where the picture of the Virgen hung on the wall with photographs stuck into the frame of her father and brothers who left the high Alpujarras "where everyone else will go". In those fifteen square metres where doors and curtains divide still further, she loved, suffered, gave birth, and raised her children to the military service and arranged marriages. There, her grand-children bustled and swarmed, away from their parents and the parents would return home when the evening church bells pealed, their arms hanging tired and exhausted.

Her husband would curve his body, continually going up and down as he lowered his head towards the earth, glimpsing the rye fields, vegetable plots, and the walley. He had learned to farm like his grandfather before him. He worked hard to harvest but reaped little, but even so would give thanks to his Lord. It is as if guardian angel reminded him always, "this plot could have been only pure starch", but it still could easily return to the wild and unproductive land it would be without his constant work. He worked for a wage which might be a half, a third, or even a quarter of the crop, sweating by the week, going from farm to farm - all made use of him.

More and more his back would bow lower. Sometimes now and then he would stand in the wide doorway of a tavern and while drinking half a bottle, he would know every grape for which he was paid and where it ripened, and every flower blooming on every stalk. He would smoke a hand-rolled cigarette and philosophise about how easy everything could have been and how difficult it was. But if we are here, here we stay and perhaps another time our path will be less steep. Do not wait forever.

One day he woke up and didn't see the sun shining through the crack in the window, and so thought, "it's over". He had kept vigil through three wakes and had prayed and they gave him white bread. This was a strong memory because communion in the Alpujarra only made use of rye bread. Wheat was for the privileged. They took him to Granada on a mule in the end. In a hospital bed and covered with sheets, he spent his last moments dreaming of the golden corn on the terraced slopes and the bell peppers swinging like pendulums, but forgot about his goat who used to eat from his hand, and his ass, the gentle brute he used to stroke and who shared his struggle, never complaining of his lot.

The generations later should come and contemplate the roman rakes, hoes, ploughs, and the rugged cliffs hanging over escarpments, the fields sown on rocky soil under them and the seed beds, hanging on these mad, dangerous cliffs. The generations to come should admire this place and the unique people of the Alpujarra who could harvest thorns and plant trees.

Emilio Fuentes Laguna

Capileira

Y SEVILLA...

*De los cuatro
puntalitos
que sostienen
a Triana
S. Jacinto,
los Remedios
La O y señá
Santana.*

SEVILLA

They constitute one of the most outstanding historical groups in the city. «The richest in the lands of Spain» in the times of the Emperor Charles. Etimologically «al-qasr» means fortified palace. There are four different parts: The mudéjar Palace of Pedro I, the *Casa de la Contratación o del Almirante* —Admiral—, Palace of Charles I and the gardens.

EL PALACIO MUDEJAR DE PEDRO I
The Mudéjar Palace of Pedro I

It possibly occupies the place of the primitive palace of the times of Pedro I, built by Mudéjares mainly come from Toledo and Granada —the Mudéjares were Moslems living in Christian kingdoms—. On the facade one reads the date 1402, which after the Gregorian readjustment,

Patio de las Muñecas

Patio de las Doncellas →

Perspectiva de los salones

Cúpula. Salón del Trono

should read 1364; it is therefore the oldest palace in use in Spain.

The entry is through a horizontal vestibule, to cut away any possible view from outside, and consequently, the inside remains protected from any strange onlookers. And one arrives at the Palacio de las Doncellas (The Maidens' Palace), those that tradition has it, the Castillians had to pay to the Moslems, when Castille was only a county. The famous «tribute of the hundred maidens». With its air almost monastical, it has something difficult to express in words, for it is a hard task to justify the East in the West. The Palace is supported by Italian columns come from the workshop of Antonio María Aprile de Carona, with stucco tracery using hands, bears and columns matched by the «plus ultra» of the King Emperor's Renaissance times.

SALON DE EMBAJADORES
Ambassadors Hall

56

It is the Alcazar's most prodigious, since it is the best preserved as well as the richest. Inside it, the king poet Al-Mutamid had his Literary Academy. On its floor fell the still warm blood of the Maestre de Santiago and there he exhaled his last breath. The unfortunate Prince Don Fadrique, who was killed for reasons still not clear to some historians. Here the Caesar Charles, unable to wait for the following day to the one scheduled for his nuptials, married Doña Isabel de Portugal «the one with the sweet speech».

Fabulous, extraordinary place, for a throne an antechamber, has the multi-secular vocation of a throne hall. Its plan is square, the flat earth, each edge represents «finis terra mundi», and the heavens is the celestial vault with its seven circles; number cabalistic and magical, as well as holy. All the cultures, civilisations and religions paid tribute to it; the days of the week, the sacraments, the candelabra. The china clay work repeats the fundamental motive

of the patio of the doncellas; but it flattens itself, and gains in colour: red, green, blue, white, yellow. Without doubt the «faithful believers» testified their Moslem beliefs in the Christain palace, « chejada, sakat, salat, ramadan, and hajj».

After having had our full of the colours, sizes, forms and gilts, when we think these cannot be overcome, we come across the opposite: small, delicate, miniature, filigree... a yard that evoques opposing sensations, contrasting and ever dissimilar. It is there; and almost excuses itself for its perfection The Patio de las Muñecas, (the Court of the Dolls), sonorous and humble, big and small. It is a dichotomy, a courtyard that would seem to be made for a harem, although officially it never was one. With its jalousies, —from jealous—, to fufil the supreme, feminine wisdom; to see without being seen. The whims of the cartesian logic say it is the smallest yard of the Alcázar, to justify its name, so accurate it needs no explanation. Its name is pure magic, the magic the Andalusians call «duende» (goblin enchanter something not at all prosaic). And the little faces of the other dolls, round cheeked and even a little ugly, mock us, for the uncautious to believe the yard is named after them.

We take a few steps and we enter the «Dormitorio del Rey Moro» (the Moorish King's Bedroom) double chamber with stucco work where praises to several personsages are written for the knowledge of posterity. As in other places of the Palace, there is an insistent iconography of castles, with triple towers and rampant lions depicting the arms that conquered the city from Moslem hands, as well as «the Orden de la Banda» (Order of the Band) with its heads of wolves joined by the dark coloured band, which Enrique IV «el de las mercedes» (The Merciful), ordered to add.

The room has an antechamber where the former motive is repeated and where once more the legend by dint of reiteration gains something in credibility. It is the antechamber room of the favourite, the predilect of the harem, who was not always the youngest or the most beautifiul, as there were gifts which were more appreciated than the ephemeral ones that last, at most, a few flowerings of the orange tree.

SALONES DEL ALMIRANTE
Admiral's Hall

It is really a wing of the Alcázar; It is also known as «La Casa de la Contratación», —sort of rudimentary Stock Exchange—, since in the first few years after the discovery of «The Indies» —America—, it was the place for doing business, and such was the bulk of the transactions that it was termed as «the richest in Spain» by the official scribe. In the «Capilla de los Almirantes», (Admiral's Chapel), Charles I gave the order to the then unknown Fernando de Magallanes to circumnavigate the world, in the year 1519; but the latter died in the enterprise. After, Juan Sebastían Elcano born at Guertaria, would take over and succeded in the year 1522, but at the cost of his health. There is «La Virgen de los Mareantes», or «del Buen Aire», (Our Lady of the Navigators or of Good Air-breeze—). By both names is known this most beautiful Spanish-Flemish panel painting by Alejo de Fernández, where it is said are represented the most important personages —the crème— of the 16th century; Colon (Columbus), los Pinzones, de la Cosa, and the Emperor himself.

In the present days the «Casa de la Contratación» finishes its repertoir with the pictures of the Spanish Roayal family, giving it a late 19th. century romantic air. Alfonso XII at Sandhurst Academy, painted over the body of Amadeo I when the King was about to come to Seville, and there was no official portrait of himself; his two wives, the Montpensiers, and his French grand parents, Louis Philippe and his wife, and Fernando VII. The shelves of fans delight all visitors; an object originally Chinese, takes a Portuguese name, and becomes definitely Spanish.

PALACIO DE CARLOS V
Charles V Palace

It is built on the oldest part of the Alcázar, over some pavilions of Fernandine times, originally Gothic, and reformed for the nuptials of the Emperor. It has three halls: that of the Tunis war tapestries, faithfully and accurately restored recently; now they can be admired in all their splendour. In ten of them the punitive expedition to the north of Africa to appease the belicose intents of the Turks at the begining of the 16th century. Special mention deserves the military parade at Barcelona's harbour, also the map of Spain orientated with the north below, which are of the Royal tapestry factory of St. Barbara, Madrid, by Jacob van der Gotten, 18th century. The chapel has pictures of indifferent quality with the exception of one early Murillo: the Miracle of St. Francis Solano at the moment of appeasing the furious bull. The third hall is the dining room, where the six horsed carriage of the Dukes of Montpensier is on show; the lamps are reproductions of others in silver disappeared during the French invasion in 1810. The painted canvases represent the departure, navigation, discovery and colonisation of America, the three famous caravelles, as well as the coat of arms of the Spanish American countries, all by M. Cañas dated 1923. There exists a fourth hall of identical size to the Chapel, but it is empty and closed to visitors. The tiles are by Cristóbal de Augusta dated in several places 1578.

JARDINES
Gardens

For the visitor with time to spare, to walk, to breathe and to get lost in these gardens is a real pleasure. Because of

Patio de las Doncellas

its privileged climate, the flora in Seville is extremely varied, where botany lovers will find a large number of flowers unknown to them. One could almost call it a botanical garden if only the numerous different species were labelled: magnolia trees, plumbagos, bowes, syringas, agapantos, clivias, zapota trees, orange trees, lemons, pomegranates, grapefruit and a long etc.

Very small buildings are scattered in these gardens.

The Charles I Pavilion deserves special mention built over a Moslem «Kubba» and «La Fuente de la Leona» (Fountain of the Lioness) by the side of the Poets' garden. These buildings give the gardens a homelike air, always guarded by the Alcázar walls and stout towers: one marvellous island of peace in the vortex of the modern city, since it occupies almost its geometrical centre.

Jardines del Alcazar

THE CATHEDRAL

On part of the grounds occupied by the old Mosque, «aljama», whose vestiges are «El Patio de los Naranjos», (Orange Tree Court), and the Giralda, the «swama», towers impressively grave and graceful, the well called «magna hispalense», since it is the third Christian cathedral, after the Vatican's St. Peter, and London's St. Paul.

It is dedicatd to «Santa María de la Sede», (Our Lady of the See). It is estimated it was built 1401-1506, as the 1388 earthquake had seriously damaged the then existing Mosque-Cathedral. The architects mentioned are; Alonso Martínez in 1472, Pedro de Toledo, Franciso Rodríguez. In 1496 Simón de Colonia and finally Juan Gil de Hontañón.

Capilla Real, (Royal Chapel) with the «virgen de los Re-yes», (Our Lady of the Kings), —patroness of the Archi-diocesis— made in larchwood, a present from St. Louis of France, to his first cousin, St. Fernando of Castille, who is buried in a prodigious silver urn, engraved by Laureano Si-món de Pina; also the tombs of Don Alfonso «el Sabio», (the Wise), and his mother, Doña Beatriz de Suabia.

La Sacristia Mayor: such is the size of this Sacristy, that Phillip II «el prudente», said to the canons, «You have a better sacristy than my Royal Chapel». Its custodian is by Arfe, dated 1587, and weighs 358.323 kgs. San Isidro and San Leandro: paintings by Murillo, 1665. The 1548 des-cent from the Cross, by Pedro de Campaña with plateres-que decorations; also an impressive candelabrum.

Capilla Mayor: This chapel possesses the largest

Christian retable. The flemish Pyeter Dancart started in 1482 and worked on it till 1492. Jorge Fernández Alemán took over and finished it in 1525. In thirty six compartments, the life, pasion and death of Jesus Christ are related; from his birth in Bethlehem to his death on Calvary it is also called «Cristo del Millón» and it has over a thousand sculptures of the late Gothic syle. All this work is gilded and this gold gives it an unparalleled richness and solemnity. Real prodigy of these craftsmen. To be mentioned the central grill and the side pulpits by the friar Francisco de Salamanca: 1532.

Coro (Choir): It follows the multisecular rule in all Castillian cathedrals; it is situated in front of the high altar. The 117 stalls are in ebony, 67 of them high and 50 low. The present organs are 1724 with Pedro de Cornejo wooden sculptures. The instruments made by Aquilino de Amezúa (1901-1903) with more than six thousand tubes. In 1973 an electronic device was incorporated.

Tumba de Cristóbal Colón (Columbus' tomb). When he died his remains in 1506 were, it would seem, sent to Santo Domingo and later to the Habana, for whose cathedral this monument was made. After the Cuban independence in 1898, the Admiral's remains were brought over to Seville, to rest definitely by the side of Our Lady of the Antigua, according to Columbus' specially expressed wish. The work is by the sculptor Arturo Mélida Alinari in 1891 and it was crowned with the heraldics of Castille, León, Navarre and Aragón.

San Antonio (St Anthony). It is really the baptistry. Outstanding the vision of St. Anthony by the Seville painter Murillo, 5.60 ms. high, done in 1656, as well as The Baptism of Christ of 1658. The painting of St. Anthony was cut up and robbed in 1865, but it was recovered a few months later by the Spanish consul in New-York. It was brought back to the Seville Cathedral and later sent to The Prado where it was restored by the Museum's first restorer Salvador Martínez Cubells.

Other chapels of interest: Our Lady of the Antigua painted on a wall portion of the orignal Mosque. The Immaculate «Chica» (Small), a Montañés work considered in its time «the finest thing in the world». The Saint Guadian Angel, another Murillo, painted between the years 1665-1669 for the Seville Capuchines and donated to the City in 1814. The St. Jame's Chapel with the Roelas canvas of St. James in the battle of Clavijo.

LA MEZQUITA DE SEVILLA
Seville Mosque

The calif Abu Yacub Yusuf started the works of the mosque «aljama». Very little still stands. The architect Ahmed Ali Inb Basso took over in the year 1172 and completed it four years later. The «quibla» was in the south part, the side which is —today— by the «Archivo de Indias» (The Indies Archives). It still reamins the «sahan», now the «Patio de los Naranjos», (Orange-tree court), for ritual washing. Notable is the «Puerta de perdón», (Pardon Door), which was the principal access to the Mosque, with some knockers in cast bronze, superbly preserved.

LA GIRALDA

It is the usual tower of the Mosques: their minaret or «swama». It was started under the Calif Abu Yusuf Ibn Baso, but it was under the Calif Abu Yusuf Yacub al Mansur, «the victorious», after his victory at the battle of Alarcos «Al-Arak», near Calatrava, over Alfonso VIII, when this colossal monument was finished, to celebrate this victory, 8th of sa'ban 591 of the Moslem calendar (18th July 1195). It has a splendid arrow on top, which was added by the Cordobese Hernán Ruiz betweeen the years 1558-1568. Also on top the statue of the Faith by Bartolomé Morell, 1568, 6.90 ms. high. It is the City's distinctive emblem. The tower measures 93.90 ms. and it possesses 25 bells; San Miguel de las Victorias is the oldest, and Santa María, of 1539, the largest. It is decorated with the Andalusian motive «Paños de Sebka».

BARRIO DE SANTA CRUZ

St. Cross Quarter

At the foot of the walls of the impressive Alcázar is located this urban jewel, where the whim is the rule and where at Rodrigo street one does not know its right width; Susona a bitter picture of a history even more bitter. Plaza de los Venerables (The Square of the Venerables) breathes, after so much narrowness, only to get even narrower at Reinoso, where the curious visitor will be able to verify what was always said in this quarter: «if you open your arms you can touch both sides of the street» and there are still arms to spare. From a window a dog will bark and from another a smell of cooking, if one goes about eleven along the «calle de la Vida» (Life). Suddenly silence... A voice, one song, but where? At the bottom of the street. We have, of course, arrived at the Plaza de Doña Elvira (Doña Elvira's Square).

We come across gipsy boys who sing rather well or not quite in tune. Stop; fifteen minutes to assimilate what the guide has said and what we have seen. Time to see and touch the local craftsmanship, from the cord that is made at Santa María la Mayor, to the handmade embroidery which is done in the villages of the provinces. We leave Doña Elvira square, and surprise! it was here where Figaro shaved his customers. The square we have just left behind was that one brought to universal fame by Rossini's «El Barbero de Sevilla». Before leaving this quarter, which was a Jewish ghetto, we shall make a fleeting stop to have a drink, and Jabugo ham. This ham is really delicious «the ham made more Christians than the Holy Inquisition». Across the little square of Alianza and Joaquín Romero we shall reach the Cathedral.

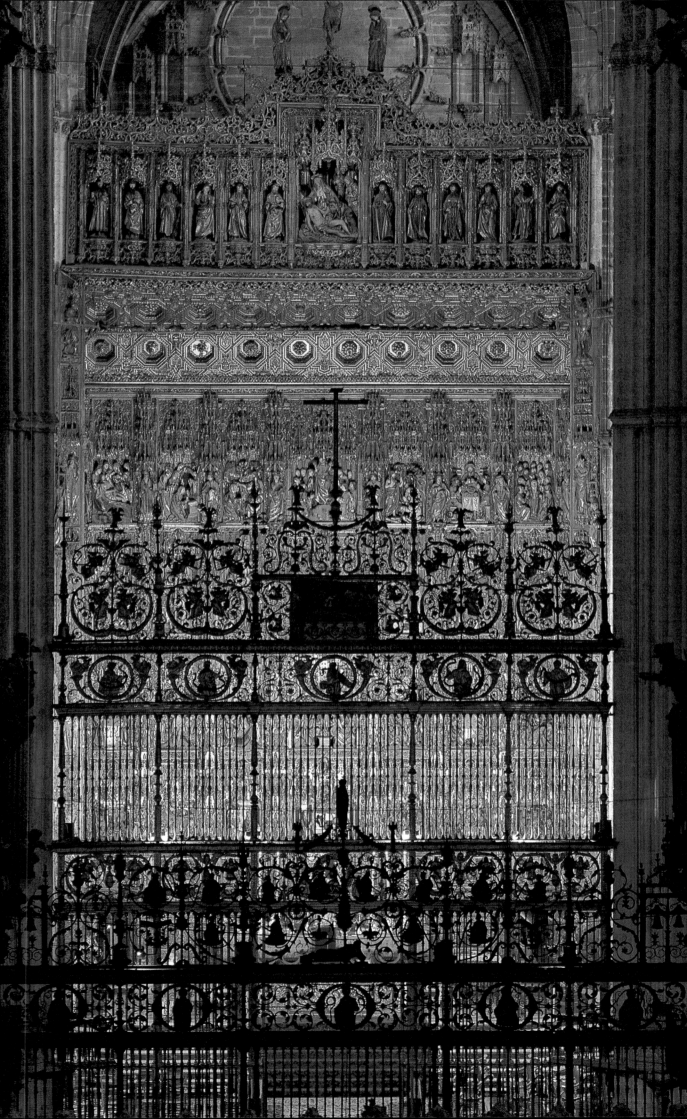

Plaza de España ←

Museo Arquelógico

VISTA PANORAMICA
(Panoramic visit)

In a brief tour through the city, if possible in a tourist bus, or car, —because of the distances to cover—, one can admire:

TORRE DEL ORO

It is as well as the Giralda the best known tower in the city, and Islam's most famous Military tower. It was built in 617 (8th March 1220). It is dodecagonal. Each side faces one of the twelve winds; Eurus, Scolans, Notus, Auster, Africus, Euroauster, Zephirus, Stannus, Irieus, Boreas, Aquilo and Volturnus.

EL GUADALQUIVIR

In the present times the only navigable river in Spain, this city being, as a consequence the only inland port in this country, it is 93 kms. from its mouth at Sanlucar de Barrameda on the Atlantic. Six hours are taken to arrive there. The name comes from the Arab «Al-Wad al Kevir», the great river.

PARQUE DE MARIA LUISA

Donated to the city by Princess Luisa Fernanda de Or-

Pabellón Mudéjar
Plaza de
América

leans Duchess of Montpensier, in the year 1893. Of considerable dimensions. In the park there are several small summer houses, dedicated to people who have left their mark in the city: the singer Ofelia Nieto, Torucato Luca de Tena, Hermanos Machado, Dante and the very notable summer house dedicated to Gustavo A. Becquer, masterpiece of the Marchena born sculptor, Lorenzo Goullaut Varela; besides the effigy of the poet, the love that wounds, and the wounded love are represented by little cupid angels, and by three maidens: the before, during, and the after love (Illusion, Plenitude and Disillusion). A work, worthy of being seen together with a gigantic yew tree planted in 1850.

PLAZA DE ESPAÑA

The best work of the architect Anibal González y Alvá-

Pabellones de
la Plaza de
España

rez-Osorio (1876-1929) in a style probably wrongly called
«historical-modernistic»; 200 ms. in diameter where the arches depict the Spanish provinces, and the bridges the
four peninsular kingdoms.

PLAZA DE AMERICA

It is called popularly —and with good reason— of the
«Palomas», (the pigeons), because of over a thousand white pigeons, that in complete freedom are found there. It is
to be noted they are all white. Its three pavilions were de-
singed by Anibal González on the occasion of the Spanish
American Fair of 1929. The three pavilions are of the three
dominating styles in Spain at the time of the discovery of
America 1492: Mudejar, (left), Gothic-Isabeline, (centre),

Detalles

and Renaissance-Plateresque, (right), where now the museums of Artes y Costumbres Populares, (popular art), Etnográfico and Arqueológico, are found.

JARDINES DE CATALINA DE RIBERA
Gardens of Catalina de Ribera

In one corner of these gardens, are located those named after Murillo; but the Seville people called them all after the name of the painter, rather than after the Marchioness of Tarifa, who was so generous to the city in the 16th

century, when at their cost the hospital of The Five Wounds was built. In the centre of the gardens there is a monument to the discovery of America.

PALACIO DE SAN TELMO
Palace of St. Telmo

This palace in 1682 was the National School for pilots and navigators trained for the voyage to South America. In 1778 it became a nautical college for young noblemen; this teaching was suppressed: in 1847. In 1849 it was

Casa de Pilatos

bought by the Dukes of Montpensier, to be used as their residence. The Duchess donated it to the Archbishopry that installed there the major seminary of the diocese in 1901. The facade is by Leonardo de Figueroa.

MURALLAS DE MACARENA
Macarena Walls

This is what is left of the superb city walls, which were unfortunaltey demolished in the last century, «to allow the development of the city». It is known that it had number-less towers and monumental doors, such as the Royal Gate, which was of Renaissance style. The names are still preserved, but not so the buildings. Bib Johar or Minjoar —Puerta de la Carne, (Gate of the Flesh); Bab Qurtuba —Puerta de Córdoba— (Gate of Córdoba); Bab Aqrmura —Puerta de Carmona— (Gate of Carmona; Baba al-ma-qabir —Puerta Osario— (Gate of the Ossuary); Bab Maqa-rana —Puerta de la Macarena— (Gate of the Macarena); Bab al Kuhl —Puerta de Goles— (Gate of Goles), degene-ration of Hergoles, and this of Hercules— or Royal Gate. Bab al-Sams —Puerta del Sol— (Sun Gate); Baba Arragel, the existing street Bibarragel; Bab Tiryana —Puerta de

Fábrica de Tabacos

Ayuntamiento

La Maestranza

Triana— (Triana Gate); Bab al-Rambla) —Puerta de la Arena— (Sand Gate); bab al-Zayt —postigo del Aceite— (wicket of the oil); Bab al-Qatai —Puerta del Carbón— (Coal Gate); and finally, a Gate universal to Seville, Bab Sris —Puerta de Jeréz— (Sherry Gate).

PLAZA DE TOROS
Bull Ring

It is one of the city's most typical buildings. The works were started in 1755 under the direction of the architect, Vicente San Martín. In 1765 the Palco del Principe, (Prince's Pavillion), was finished by the Portuguese, Cayetano de Acosta, in honour of the Spanish Prince, Don Felipe de Borbón, Prince of Parma, and son of Felipe (Philip V). It has a capacity for 13.934 spectators. It is egg-shaped, 63 m by 57.50 m.

It has 118 asymmetrical balconies; the widest 2.58 m. and the smallest, and narrowest, 1.84 m. In front of the Puerta del Principe (Prince's Door) the other side of the Paseo de Colón, there is a modest statue to one of the universal myths of the city: «Carmen».

AYUNTAMIENTO
Town Hall

The idea of starting the works on a new site was proposed in 1526 to celebrate the nuptials of Charles V —before it was at the «Corral de los Olmos» attached to the Cathedral, the actual square «Virgen de los Reyes», (Our Lady of the Kings)—. The works are by Diego de Riaño who worked at them between 1527-1534; Apeadero, Sala de Cabildo, (Corporation Hall), and the façade on the Plaza de S. Francisco, (St. Francis' Square).

Besides all that has been said, Seville does not end here. We can mention La Iglesia del Hospital de la Caridad, (Charity Hospital), and its private collection of Murillo's masterpieces. La Casa de Pilatos the palace of the Dukes of Medinaceli; its true name being, the Palace of San Andrés, (St. Andrew). The basilica of Nuestra Señora de la Esperanza, «Macarena», (Our Lady of Hope), where all the year a throne of Seville's Holy Week is on show.

Besides Seville is not to be written about or photographed. One touches and feels Seville in the spring and summer nights of the «Barrio de Santa Cruz».

Pablo Morán

75

Itálica.

*Córdoba lejana
y sola...
G. Lorca*

*Si quieres venir,
te vienes
a Cordobita
la llana
que están
los cambios
de trenes.*

CORDOBA

THE MOSQUE CATHEDRAL OF CORDOBA

Córdoba lies in the wide Guadalquivir valley formed between mountains of the Primary and Tertiary era, or Alpine movement.

A settlement in prehistoric times chosen for its privileged geographical situation, the town was founded by the Roman pretor Marcus, Claudius Marcelus in 169 BC. as a patrician colony, later to become capital of the Roman province of Betica.

Once the Roman unity was broken, Córdoba lived under Visigoth rule, continuing the decadent Roman system for the three centuries since it had been so powefully absorbed.

In 711 the Hispanic world changed. Visigoth disruption justified the Muslim invasion from North Africa, integrating the Iberian Peninsular in the Islamic world as Al Andalus, an emirate, subject to Damascus, with cordoba as capital from 716.

Abd ar Rahman, «the emigrant», a prince from the fallen Omeyad dinasty, supplaned by the Abbasies, proclaimed in 756 the independence of Western Islam, reigning as Abd ar Rahman I. Of intelligent and energetic character he made Muslim Spain a strong and organised state.

A royal court or «jassa», began to develop in the appointed capital, Córdoba. As it grew it became necessary to build an «Aljama» (main) Mosque.

Construction started in 785 on a small promontory over the Guadalquivir, on a site already sacred in other religions. Occupied by a Visigoth hermitage to St. Vincent, used by Muslims as a Mosque, and according to local scholars, a Roman temple, where since the 2nd. century BC. the Gods were invoked for victory. This theory is based on the discovery of two columns with an inscription to Janus Agustus; now exposed in the «Patio de los Naranjos», (Orange Tree Court).

82

Galería Norte del patio.

The building of all mosques begins with the «Kibla» wall facing Mecca, Mohammed's birthplace in 569, prilgrim centre on the Red Sea.

Mosque and Aljama are words of Arabic orig i n; the first indicating a place of worship, the second, meeting or assembly.

This city of the Kaaba is situated 45° S.E. of Córdoba, but our Mosque was built 28° S.E., a difference of 17°. Don Claudio Sańnchez Albornoz attributes the inexactness to the wall of the old hermitage being reused.

The only «Aljama» Mosque left in Spain, after a long period of Muslim domination, it is also one of the largest in the world. The South facade measures 128 m. from N. to S. and is 175 m. long, approximately 22.400 squ.m. The measuring unit was the cubit, exactly 47.5 cms. in the Mirhab.

It is mostly built in a local fosilifeorus limestone, «piedra franca», very sensitive to natural erosion, (by rain, wind and temperature changes).

The façades are straight and severly cut by buttresses and crowned by sharply angled battlements of eastern origin, it appears the Fort of the Faith.

Three parts form the Mosque: minaret, ablutions or purification court, and covered prayer room.

We know the location of the earliest minaret from Hisam I. discovered in the «Patio de los Naranjos», by Don Felix Hernández. It was 23.5 m high. Abd ar Raham II made another in the 10th. century nearly double in superimposed cubic bodies, the smaller above, were covered by a semiespherical dome, topped by an iron rod with several spheres.

There were separate flights of steps to ascend and descend. Starting from the eastern and western sides they converge South at the top, where five times every day, the

muezzin called the faitfhul to pray from the four cardinal points.

The last repairs to the tower ended in 1763 after the Lisbon earthquake. The third body of the tower houses twelve bells and the fourth a clapper, that substitutes the bells in Holy Week, also a clock with two bells. The syle is Renaissance touched with Herrerian details.

All mosques have an open courtyard for ablution rituals; Muslims believe the senses are «gates of the hell», so carefully wash before entering the prayer hall.

The present dimensions of this yard date back to the late 19 century, when Al Mansur enlarged it. The name «Patio de los Naranjos» (Orange Tree Court) derives from orange trees recorded since the 15th century. Before there were palm trees, Olive trees and cypresses were planted in the 18th century.

Originally water was taken from a well by a water wheel. Later, the second caliph Al Haken II had mountain streams channelled to the ablution fountains, also lost.

The cistern from Al Mansur's times, with 600.000 litres capacity, still exits, though in disuse. Today there are five fountains, the largest «The Olive Spring» and the smallest are 18th century and the three grilled mudéjar ones 15th century.

The court is flanked by covered galleries except in the prayer hall where nineteen archways open to the interior; the broadest towards the «mihrab».
towards the «mirhab».

It is difficult to imagine from the outside the unusual interhal distribution formed by assimetric disposition and variety of elements.

Once inside, one can perceive an atmosphere of light, temperature, through the forest of columns, capitals and bicoloured arches, but above all, there is an overwhelming sense of religious mistery that speaks of a site of constant worship, a mysitc aura which imposes silence.

The most outstanding feature is the double arched colonnade to raise the height of the ceilings. Strong round

La MEZQUITA

AMPLIACIÓN DE ALHAKEN II

AMPLIACIÓN DE ABDERRAMAN II

AMPLIACIÓN DE ALMANZOR

MEZQUITA ORIGINAL DE ABDERRAMAN I

PATIO DE LOS NARANJOS

Nave central desde las arquerías del lucernario. Al fondo, la Macsura.

arches over branching horseshoe arches, that serve as flying buttresses out towards the walls, alternating red brick, and white limestone wedges.

The columns, base, shaft, and capital, are from earlier buildings of other cultures.

All are different sizes, materials, —various coloured marbles, granite, and alabaster—, and shapes, plain, straight, fluted or spiral.

Columns were adapted to regulate the arcade's height, cutting shafts, or adding larger or smaller capitals and bases. Each has independent foundations.

The eight aisles are perpendicular to the «kibla» wall,

Ampliación de Abderrahman II, capitel y fuste de alabastro.

important element of mosque construction, fully established since Córdoba.

In Abd ar Rahman's first Mosque every row of columns had twelve double arches. The floor was mortar made from chalk, water and sand, dyed with red iron oxide. Contempory Macael (Almería) marble floor tiles date from the restoration of 1920.

A flat wooden ceiling of beams and plancs was covered by a gable roof over each nave, that channeled rainwater to inner ducts through the walls.

Light penetrated from the outside courtyard, reflecting arches and floor to the «kibla» wall, where some oil lamps burned to attract the attention of the Faithful. A stone altar decorated with geometric designs of late Roman influen-

Cúpula gallonada de la Macsura, con mosaico bizantino.

ce, and a mutilated stone cross, are left from Visigoth times.

Political and economic development under Abd ar Rahman II, and a subsequent increase in population, caused the emir to enlarge the Mosque.

Work began in 833, destroying the first «kibla» wall, and continuing the eleven naves with eight arches. As before building materials were reused permitting a quick but strong building structure. The old pattern was repeated, except for the columns had no base and eleven of the capitals were purposely made by Cordobese craftsmen. They were in a design inspired in the Corinthian model and nearing the future honeycomb sytle so charactristic of the future Caliphate periods.

Much of this part was modified by the Cathedral transept.

Abd ar Rahman III proclaimed himself first Omeyad Caliph in the west under the title of «the Victorious» in 929, after subduing the sons of Omar ben Hafsum in Al Andalus, the fatimites in North Africa and pacifying his northern frontiers with the Christian kingdoms. Córdoba, then, lived its maximun splendour in peace and prosperity.

The first Caliph concentrated on building the royal city of Medina Azahara, where new oriental traits appear and develop into the Cordobese Caliphate style.

Al Haken II completed Medina Azahara in 926 and, prompted by demografic increase, undertook another enlargement of the Mosque the same year.

This difficult task was solved by master architects, who without breaking the structural unity, added some innovating effects to the already flowering Cordobese art.

Once again the «kibla» wall was pulled down and the eleven naves lengthened, this time with twelve more arches. Specially carved columns have rose veined or dusky

Cúpula esquilfada en la Macsura.

blue marble shafts, no base. Capitals are inspired in the Corinthian or Compound order. Along the central nave eight solid pilasters are decorated with geometric motifs; on the lower part double embellishments; on the higher, patterns deriving from the Corinthian of Compound order. Above these cuffic scripts, (koranic verses).

The ceiling, according to Idrisi, of Tortosa pine wood, was flat over transverse beams. It was richly carved and beautifully painted.

A definite feature of the new style arose from the lighting problem. Light from the far away open court yard was insufficient, so domed skylights were designed. The first, over the main nave, enhances the way to the Mihrab giving it a spacial air.

As the domes were made of stone, they were much heavier than the wooden ones. It was therefore necessary to build thick walls to support them like in Romanesque contemporary Europe. The difference was that the Cordobese architects, when designing the first skylight, created a different supporting system, forming groups of columns which support inter crossing arches, real nets that reinforce the construction and allow a better visibility to the South wall where the Mihrab is found.

The lower half horseshoe arch, now free from weight, is transformed into another of five lobules. On the arches, other new horseshoe ones rest, which substitute the old round ones.

From the keystones of the festooned arches, begins other similar arches that cross the horseshoe ones, and spread the weight to other points, transmitting the load to the ground by way of the columns.

The dome has eight ribs, four parallel to the four sides,

four smaller cross ribs, starting from the middle of the sides and passing throught the intersection of the first. Eight latticed windows appear on the lower part of the dome between the ribs.

Few times have architecture and geometry kept such balance and closeness.

After the conquest of Córdoba by St. Ferdinand in 1236, and the consecration of the covered part of the temple as cathedral, under the advocation of «Santa María la Mayor», by Don Juan, bishop of Osma, it was necessary to adopt it to the new cult, using the best lighted part as chancel, by placing a High Altar there.

In 1257 don Fernando de Mesa, Bishop of Córdoba makes the Altar rest over the East side arches, adopting Gothic forms today disappeared; and this way orientated the Christian prayers towards Jerusalem.

As these columns, partially, prevented full visibility of the Altar the bishop Don Iñigo Manrique, had some arches pulled down: four rows the length of three arches. In their place a new Gothic panelled nave was built. The new walls have stained glass windows at the top part, and the back wall is decorated with a rosette.

On the floor, fifty one memorial stones are found; we can mention that of Don Pedro de Zeballos Cortés y Calderón, first Spanish vice-roy of the provinces of Plata (Argentine today).

The Capilla Real, (Royal Chapel), or of St. Ferdinand, is attached to the Villaviciosa Chapel. This «Capilla Real» is of small rectangular shape covered by a dome; which follows the same pattern as the former: the naves and the spaces between them, being adorned with Mozarabe stucco tracery work. The walls above, present the same work, but Almohade, and on the lower part has similar decorations but of ulterior date.

The tiled wainscot is of Enrique II time. During a long period it was used as a funeral chapel; in the crypt were buried the remains of the Castille Kings, Alfonso XI, «el Justiciero», (the Just), and Ferdinand IV; they were, at a la-

ter date, moved to the Real Colegiata de San Hipólito.

Several scholars maintain the chapel dates back to Al Mansur times, where following the tradition of the great mosques a «Dakka» (platform) would have been installed; from it the «Mousammi» would repeat the Friday's prayer to the Faithful scattered about the temple.

The «Macsura» represents the summit of the Caliphate architecture. Situated in the centre of the «kibla» wall, it is the space between the «mihrab» and the faithful, and was generally reserved to the Caliph and his courtiers.

In this case it is made of three cuadrangular spaces, closed by skylighted domes. These, follow the same trend as those of the Villaviciosa chapel.

In the central, of larger dimensions, the round nerves which intercross one another form an octagonal lantern dome. Nevertheless, in the smaller sized domes, the nerves intercross once again, but they draw in the centre, an eight pointed star, and the octagon thus formed is closed by a dome.

A great arch in the centre of the «Mascura», under the principal dome, gives access to the «Mihrab», which, embedded in the wall, is of regular octagonal design. The wainscot is in streaked white marble, with relief cuffic inscriptions at the top. Above, and supported by ornamental rests, runs a white marble cornice finely decorated; once again Koran texts appear.

Six blind trebled arches supported by small marble columns, with Caliphate capitals, decorate the higher part. The spaces between the arches are Damaskeen work.

The «Mihrab» is covered by a plaster shell shaped dome.

The decoration of the arch leading to the «Mihrab» show on its wainscot magnificent white marble pieces, chiselled with motifs referring to the Tree of Life.

Small cuffic inscriptions on the impost of the arch tell us the date of completion: 965.

The top part is decorated with Byzantine mosaics, glass

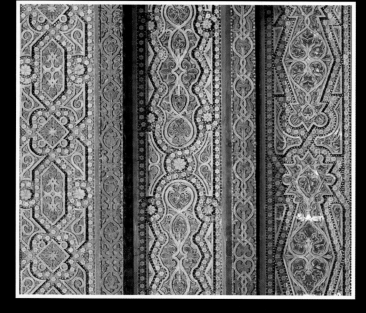

tessellated and small, alteranting coloured and gilded ones. The colours most used are purple, yellow, light green, blue, white and black. The base is gilded covered with colourless glass.

The keystones of the arch, the seven small blind arches and the central dome, were adorned with Eastern leafy motifs. On the other hand the great «alfiz» has double cubic epigraphs referring to Koranic «Suras».

It is to be noticed that for the first time in the Mosque, stucco tracery decoration appears: a precedent of the future Nazarite and Mudéjar sytle.

On the jambs of the main arch and forming its support, there are two columns, each side, with handsome marble capitals, which were moved from the «Mihrab» during the works under Abd ar Rahman II.

To the right and left of the «Mihrab», the doors of «Al Sabat» and «Bayt Al-Mal» are respectively located; their arches are decorated with the same type of mosaic. The drawings are somewhat more complicated, following the traditional Cordobese style; here again cuffic characters. Over the decoration of each door, there is a rectangular jalousie window.

As a result of the transformation of the Mosque into a Cathedral, some altar pieces or retables, covered for some time the original decoration. Under the direction of the French architect Don Baltasar de Dreventon in 1771, some

restoration work took place; worthy of note being the consolidation of the outside of the dome.

New restorations, from the year 1815 pulled down the retables, so that the mosaics could come to light. These appear greatly damaged. The Chapter of the Cathedral entrusted the organ maker Don Patricio Furrier with the execution of this work. This, he did by using small stained glass squares. Other times just glass on the paint.

The mosaic that decorates the left side was totally new, copying the ones on the right door. These works were directed by the architec Don Ricado Velázquez Bosco in 1916, and carried out by the hand of Señor Morolin, craftsman of the «Maumejean» house in Madrid.

The passage door of «Al-Sabat» communicated directly the Omeiad Alkazar with the «Macsura», throught a gallery that in the «Kibla» wall occupied the five naves from the «Mihrab» westwards, leading to the street and stretching as far as the Caliph's palace. A great arch, dismantled in the 18th century by order of the bishop Mardones, joined this passage with the residence of the Caliph.

The «Bayt Al-Mal» or treasury door gave access to the five halls situated in the «Kibla»; from the «Mihrab» to the eastern wall, where another door, called today of the «Chocolate», opened into the street. In one of these halls, and according to Idrisi, the Mosque treasure was guarded consisting in gold and silver vases, the chandelabra for the

CRUCERO DE
LA CATEDRAL:
—Detalles de la nave,
cúpula y coro.
—Ara visigótica

27th Ramadan night, and, contained in a polychromed case, a copy of the Koran; four of the pages were, before, written by the Caliph Uthman Ben Affan and stained with his blood. This Book was regularly used for the Fridays main prayer.

As in all Aljama Mosques the Cordobese Omeyad had to the right of the «Mihrab» a pulpit like «Mimban»; on it rested the Sacred Book. It was in very fine woods with mother of pearl encrustations.

To make the nobler parts of the «Macsura» more evident, from the lanterns hung three large oil lamps.

An increase in population as well as the desire to attract to his side the «Alfaquies», prompted Al Mansur in 978 to enlarge, once again, the Great Mosque. The architects did not dare to destroy the incomparable master work carried out in the south wall under the second Omeyad Caliph; because of the steep drop of the grounds towards the river and the proximity of the very river, the only possibility of amplification was to one of the side walls. As the old Alkazar was situated if front of the western wall, there was no other alternative but to enlarge the Mosque eastwards; this zone was occupied by the «Medina», and the Primer Minister was, therefore, constrained to expropiate the near buildings indemnifying the owners. This new stage of construction added eight naves to the east of the Mosque, and the courtyard, also, grew in the same proportion. As a result of these works the «Mihrab» was left out of the centre, the same as the main nave. This entailed a loss of symmetry which was sacrificed to give larger proportions to the Mosque.

To communicate the already built parts with the new naves, the old outside wall was opened by means of great horseshoe arches.

The shafts, capitals and tops, continue to be chiselled by Cordobese craftsmen, but not so finely as before. The wedges are of limestone, and painted with red and white.

The North and South walls, in this period, are of reduced widths. The building of the arches started at the same time from both sides; this caused a breach in the harmony of the group. to solve this, new arches were built; these of smaller dimensions: horseshoe, lanceolate and trebled.

When in the 18th century the roof was repaired, to give better illumination, the old panelled ceiling was substituted with skylights resting on the top of the arches. Worthy of special mention are two lanterns per nave, placed at the ends, which largely increase the illumination of the temple.

Seven doors in the new East facade led to the outside; their decorations follow traditional patterns, but already showing some signs of decadence.

To give good light to the temple, specially for the last prayer of the day, and, also for the 27th. day of the Ramadan, many lamps of several shapes and dimensions were used, some of copper or brass, and some of silver. The bigger ones had small lamps made of clay or glass, with oil and wick. They hung from the middle of the domes, arches and ceilings.

The three great lamps that hung from the lanterns of the «Macsura» were of silver, to call the attention of the Fainthful, by the scintillating of the light on the mosaics.

Arcada interior.

When Don Alonso Marinque occupied the Córdoba Episcopal See, he requested the chief stone mason of the Cathedral, Hernán Ruiz, «el Viejo» (the Old), the planning of a Major Chapel, in accordance with the trends of the times; and to locate it in the middle of the Prayer Hall, it was necessary to dismantle a great part of the work done under Abd ar Rahman and Al Mansur.

Later, in April of 1523 the works of the «Capilla Mayor» were started, without the previous consent of the Cathedral Chapter, who was forced to obey the Bishop's will.

At a Córdoba council meeting it was agreed to stop the destructive work, since it had been done without Royal permission. Later on, the works continued, although the «Corregidor» (Mayor), and the Municipal Council, passed an order, threatening with the death penalty, those that destroyed the Mosque without Royal consent. The following day the Bishop excommunicated the «Corregidor», who took the matter to the King. The King ruled in favour of the Cathedral Chapter, and ordered the work to be resumed.

Rumour has it, that when King Charles I went through Córdoba, after his wedding to his cousin, Isabel of Portugal, he visited the Cathedral and exclaimed: «I did not know what this was, otherwise I would not have allowed the old part to be changed; because what you are doing can be done elsewhere, whereas you have destroyed something that was unique in the world».

After all the problems were overcome, the works were continued by Hermán Ruiz, «El Viejo». He adapted the works to the previous Mosque sytle, and accomplished the task of combining such different trends.

The merge was so perfect, that the Mosque main nave goes through the new works, without preventing the sight of the «Mirhab». Notwithstanding this, when the observer, positioned under the dome, looks from the transept at the closing East wall, the nave cannot be seen, as this has been absorbed by other parts of the temple.

The transept structure, in the form of a Latin cross, is of late Gothic design, with great open pillars and vaults. The main nave from East to West, occupies, with its five arches, the amplification of Abd ar Rahman II, from the central axis as far as the division wall, which is broken; goes across the transept, penetrating, also, in this third and last amplification, and connecting better the two parts. From North to South it takes the space of two naves, and the creation of an elliptical dome was necessary.

After his father's death Hernán Ruiz II carried over the works until his death in 1582.

A great retable was started in 1618, following the planning of the Jesuit brother Alonso Matias, who directed the work himself.

The materials used were bronze and marble, from the quarries of Cabra, Carcabuey, and Luque; towns situated south of the Province, at the foot of the Sub-betic mountain range.

Several divergencies, during the construction, between the Company of Jesus and the author, compelled the latter to give up his work. José Luis González, who up to that time, had only been in charge of the ornamentation, took over.

In 1628 the retable was finished by Juan de Aranda. At a later date the tabernacle was added, by Sebastián Vidal, after the original drawing of the Master, Matias.

Occupying the bottom of the Chancel, it comprises a platform and two vertical bodies, forming three ways. The two small doors on either side of the platform lead to the sacristry. In the middle of the platform and under the tabernacle is the sacrarium. Four ridged columns consitute the supports of the first body; the capitals have bronze encrustations.

On the canvases are represented, St. Acisclo, on the right, and St. Vitoria on the left, Roman martyrs, the citiy patrons.

The tabernacle is placed in the centre passage; its architecture has two over and under bodies. The first is

square, and the second round, and supports a dome with marble encrustations, over which rests a handsome lantern.

A fine cornice, with rectangular centre, divides the two parts of the retable, the four pedestals on top corresponding with the four columns underneath. Between the centre columns, and in a lintelled frame, canvas represents the Annunciation of Our Lady, to whom the chapel is consecrated.

The frontal, or pedimen that crowns the ensemble has the image of God the Father, by Matias Conrado.

The eight stone figures covered in bronze were carved by pedro Freyre de Guevara.

The author of the paintings was the Bujalance artist Acisclo Antonio Palomino.

Under the Epistle pulpit there is a sculpture of an angel, resting on a lion. These four figures represent, according to Christian tradition, the Evangelists, whose writings constitute the foundations of the Christian Faith. The cupolas are also in mahogany; on them rest two elegant sculptures.

The vault of the chancel follows Gothic-Reanissance styles, also the cupolas of the transept; the nerves are richly ornamented.

In the presbyterian, on the Epistle side, is the kneeling statue of the bishop, the friar Diego de Mardones. He had financed the work of the retable. On the Gospel side is an equestrian statue of St. James.

On the sides of the transept an exuberant plateresque decoration impregnated with Gothic motifs, ornaments

the walls. These, underneath, are open, communicating with the rest of the Mosque.

In the intersections of the transept with the chancel, stand out two beautiful mahogany pulpits, by Miguel de Verdiguier. That on the Gospel side is erected over a rose jasper ox, which rests on a white marble cloud, with a black marble eagle by it.

Under the Epistle pulpit there is a sculpture of an angel, resting on a lion. These four figures represent, according to Christian tradition, the Evangelists, whose writings constituyte the foundations of the Christian Faith. The cupolas are also in mahagony; on them rest two elegant sculptures.

A silver votive lamp hangs over the High Altar. It was worked by the Cordobese silver smith, Martín Sánchez de la Cruz, and it measures 1.82 ms. in diameter, and weighs 200 kgs.

The impressive oval dome of Italian influence, in stucco tracery work was finished in 1600. It seems to reflect the existence in Cordoba of two stucco craftsmen schools. It has sixteen arches, adorned with small statues of bishops and saints; the Holy Trinity constitutes the key.

The choir vault is decorated with Renaissance style characters. According to Don Pedro de Madrazo, it is a vault crossed by four big skylights. Betwee these, one sees paired caryatids which support them.

All along the central part are statues of saints, placed on the stucco with intermediate adornments.

The great arches support the side walls under the dome.

99

The choir stalls deserve special mention, as the most important work of Don Pedro Duque Cornejo y Roldan. The author started to work very young in the workshop of his grandfather, the great carver Don Pedro Roldan. A learned man, with evident Baroque training, he was the most prolific sculptor of the 18th. century. When Philip V and Isabel de Farnesio visited Seville, he was appointed the Queen's Royal image maker.

In February of the year 1748 work on the 109 Cuban mahogany chairs was started. The design of the chair is rectangular, crowing the whole complex a high frontal, where the throne of the prelate is positioned. Right and left of this, separated by two small exit doors, fifty three chairs stretch each side in two rows. The Episcopal throne has three chairs, the centre for the bishop, and one on each side for the two Cathedral main dignitaries. These, at the top, are decorated with scenes of Our Lord's Ascension; the author, wishing to depict the ways to salvation, has a statue of the mystic: St. Teresa, right, and the ascetic represented by St. Mary Magdalen, left. The image of St. Raphael custodian of the city, finishes the frontal. All these statues are natural size.

On the high chairs, the great medallions on the right side show the life of Jesus Christ; those on the left represent Our Lady's. All this seems to convey Redemption themes. Below the great medallions are smaller ones, with Old Testament scenes. On the pews the medallions reproduce Cordobese martyrs.

The four angles are occupied with Gospel scenes. At the end of the stalls there are two pendulum clocks, in mahogany cases, engraved with the cursing of Adam and Eve by God.

The author died in 1757 without seeing his work finished. His sons and disciples took over in 1758; this date is engraved on one of the clocks. His mortal remains are

since 1951 at the entry of the temple. A funeral stone confirms this.

Two great organs, located by the sied walls, over the stalls, date back to the 17th. and 18th centuries, but they have undergone several alterations. The last restorations of importance were done at the beginning of the 19th century. Now they are electronic.

Bronze grills enclose the access to the choir, placed in 1759, work of the Lucema craftsman, Antonio García.

In the «Kibla» wall is the chapel of St. Teresa, also called «del Cardenal Salazar», Cordoba bishop, who at the beginning of the 18th century, ordered the constructions.

Of octagonal design and baroque decoration by Francisco Hurtado Izquierdo, it is covered with a half orange shaped cupola, with several windows below.

In a jasper and marble retable is found an image of St. Teresa, carving of the Granada artist José de Mora. Over shelves, by the same author, eight images of saints, founders and reformers of religious orders.

Acisclo Antonio Palomino was entrusted with the painting of three great pictures on Cordoba themes: the Conquest by Fernando III of Castile, the martyrdom, in the 3rd century, of the City patrons, Acisclo and Victoria; the apparition, in the 16th. century of the Archangel Raphael, to Father Roelas.

Over the side doors, there are two anonymous paintings representing the Immaculate, and the Assumption.

The sepulchre of the Cardinal represents him praying, all of it supported by six resting lions. In the front part his Ecclesiastical insignia is placed, as also the funeral inscription. This chapel was built on purpose to serve as a Major Sacristy.

The Cathedral treasure is guarded in the Sacristy, an interesting collection of gold and silver work; a considerable part of this came from Cordobese workshops.

On the shelves several pieces are on show: stoops, chalises, reliquary, jugs, lecterns and Holy Mass wine and water jars of different styles.

Among others outstand: the oldest piece, a Romanesque style crucifix (13th century) belonging ot the staff of Don Lope de Filero, first bishop of Cordoba after the Reconquest.

A reliquary bust of St. Ursula of the 15th century in engraved gilded silver.

A most beautiful Immaculate made in the 18th century by the roman silversmith Rosconi.

The most important work of art is th Great Custodia made by the silversmith of german origin Enrique de Arfe. It was taken out for the first time in the 1518 Corpus Christi procession. It was done by order of the bishop Don Martín Fernando de Angulo, between the years 1510 and 1516. Elaborated basically in silver and gilded silver, using foundry and engraving techniques. It is 2,62 ms tall and weighs over 122 kgs. This Custodia has four parts: a regular dodecagonal base, a small chapelet, Assumption chapelet and Bell chapelet. The style is late Gothic showing northern Europe influences.

An image of St. Raphael, and other of Our Lady dè la Candelaria (Candlemas) 18th century, works by the great silversmith Damian de Castro, elaborated in engraved gilded and polychromed silver.

By the same artist a beautiful sacrarium-tabernacle dated 1617 and used in the Holy Week Monument.

And last, a 16h century ivory crucifix of exquisite work, anonymus.

Among the numberless master pieces, which as a result of the alteration in the small temple, are in the premises, deserve speciali mention: Chapel of the Blessed Sacrament, with decorations by the Italian painter Cesare de Arbassia (16th century). Chapel of the Immaculate (17th century) with works of the sculptor José de Mena. Chapel «de las Animas» (Holy Souls), in which the remains of the famous historian and poet the Spanish-Peruvian Inca Garcilaso de la Vega are buried. Chapel of St. Bartholomew, with the tomb of the creator of the «culteranismo» —affected literary style— the Cordobese poet Luis de Góngora y Argote. Altar of the Annunciation, with an impressive panel painting, Flemish Spanish, work of Pedro de Córdoba executed in the 15th century. The great canvas coming from the disappeared chapel of the Last Supper, painted by Pablo de Céspedes.

101

Translated jointly by:
M. J. López and
T. D. Dobson

OTHER MONUMENTS

EL ALCAZAR DE LOS REYES CRISTIANOS
(The Alkazar of the Christian Kings)

The Spanish word Alcazar comes from the Arabic Al-Qasr, which means palace-fortress.

The Córdoba Alkazar was started in 1328, under the king Alfonso XI «el Justiciero», (The Just), on a part of the grounds formerly occupied by the Caliph's palace.

The works followed Gothic-Christian patterns. There remains the original western wall, as is shown by the vestiges of a gate. It measured 4.000 square meters, and was of rectangular ground plan.

Totally fortified, it has four towers at the corners, three of them original, and the other reconstructed.

The main tower called, «Del Homenaje», (homage), to the north east is of octagonal plant; north west a square one, «De los Leones», (lions). In front of it, the round tower called, «de la Inquisición». The tower of «La Paloma» is placed to the south east, and has recently been reconstructed.

It was a royal residence untill 1492, when after the conquest of Granada by the Catholic Kings, these donated the Córdoba alkazar to the Holy Inquisition, who established their see there.

At present several pieces of Roman times can be admi-red: an impressive marble sarcophagus, —3rd. century—, as well as a series of tessellated mosaics. And some magnificent gardens of Arab-andalusian tradition, where characteristic species of the local flora can be admired.

EL BARRIO DE LA JUDERIA
(Jewish Ghetto)

Córdoba, like other Spanish cities, had, since remote times, a Jewish community. This ethnic group reached its maximum splendour during the Caliphate. Humanists, administrators, and merchants, they were of the utmost importance to the Muslim state, and their influence continued after the downfall of it.

Placed by the wall, some part of the 14th. century Jewish ghetto —when already its size had considerably diminished—, is still standing.

The streets are narrow, hidden, twisty, with forged iron bars, through which one can see shady whitewashed courtyards, enhanced by red geraniums and green ferns, where the bubbling of little fountains make silence become music.

In its narrow central street, called, «de los Judíos», which connects the «Amodóvar» gate with «Maimónides»

square, have been found a «Mihkve», or Jewish bath, and the Synagogue, the only preserved in Andalucía. Of Mudéjar style, it has stucco tracery work of great beauty, alternating floral and geometrical decorations with Hebrew inscriptions. Small in size the access is through a small courtyard, which leads to a sort of atrium; over this there is the ladies platform. The Prayer Hall, in front of the door, is of almost square ground plan. In the eastern wall there is a great cavity, where the scrolls of «Thorah» were placed. To the left of this an original inscription indicates the construction date: 1315, under the direction of the Italian architect Isacc Moheb.

After the expulsion of the Jews, it underwent several changes, untill 1885, when it was declared National Monument.

A short distance from the Synagogue, in the Tiberiades Square, there is a great sitting sculpture, erected in 1964 to the memory of Moisés Ben Maimón, (Maimónides), the greatest Cordobese humanist of the 12 th. century.

Vista aérea y diversos detalles de la Dar al Yund y el Salón de Abderrahmán III.

MEDINA

T oday archaelogical site, it was in the 10th century, one of the most important of the palatial cities, and beautiful of the world: «Ciudad Brillantísima», is the literal translation of its name.

Due to the growth of the Caliphate Administration, the Omeyad Alkazar was insufficient to have all the new services. The Alcázar amplification being impossible because of the vicinity of the Mosque, it was necessary to dispose of another space capable of accommodating this new Administration without the limitations inherent to all cities. The new construction was situated eight kilometers north west of the city, on the lower ranges of the Sierra Morena.

The works started in 936 under Abd ar Rahman III, adapting them to the orography of the land. The consequence was a series of stepped terraces enclosed by double defensive walls.

On the highest terrace the «Dar al Mulk», or Royal Alkazar was built, as symbol of power and ownership; the «Dar al Yund», (army head quarters), separated from the royal

ZAHARA

rooms by orchards and gardens. To the east of these a great gate gave access to the ensemble.

On the middle terrace, there are several halls, among them Abd ar Rahman III's, reconstructed in 1944, by the architect and archaelogist Don Félix Hernández. This work was possible because of the great amount of well preserved remains found in the excavations; it is also called, «Salon de Embajadores». Built between the years 953 and 957 the structure is divided in three naves supported by horseshoe arches. It has rectangular chambers on both sides. The decoration is rich with stucco work, leafy forms, damaskeen work and honeycomb and latticed Caliphate capitals, on veined rose and black marble shafts. In front of these halls there were impressive gardens. A great pavilion occupied the centre, surrounded by four pools.

Mosque, houses, «Ceca», (mint), public baths, kilns, furnaces, inn, «zoco», (market), etc. were placed on the lower terrace.

The construction, —the religious style prevailing over the palatial one—, lasted till the year 961. Later, Al Haken

Averroes y murallas de la ciudad.

ll modified and enlarged it. Towards 1010, as a consequence of intestine fighting, the Caliphate disappeared, and Medina Azahara was severly damaged by Berber troops. Nevetheless, a certain life went on in the place, untill it was definitely destroyed in the 12th. century.

After a long period of oblivion, in 1854, due to some archaelogical excavations, the location of Medina Azahara was definitely found. In 1911 regular excavations to recover the city started. In 1923 the first expropriations took place. The total surface is 112 hectares, of which not yet a ten per cent has been excavated.

LUIS ALVAREZ MORENO
SALVADOR ELIAS CARABAÑO
ENRIQUE FERNANDEZ SERRANO

Translation:
M.J. López
T.D. DOBSON

Torre Calahorra
y Maimónides

107

Jaén.

JAEN

Located between Castille and Andalucía, Jaén has something in common with them both without loosing its identity. Half table land and half mountain, it has the Sierras (Mountain ranges) Morena and Del Cambrón to the north, to the south the Sub-Betic ranges, to the east the Sierra del Segura and to the west Córdoba and the low Andalucía. The river Guadalquivir, that springs in its ranges, discourses through the whole province from end to end and the olive trees embellish half its lands.

The Jaén landscapes are unmistakable: over grayish or brown hills, armies of olive trees in perfect green and silver formation, tell us of the agricultural vocation of the hard working inhabitants. The olive tree —typical of Mediterranean countries— abounds in these lands since in the 19th century the large landed properties (latifundios) became the rule. Jaén produces more and better quality olive oil than any other Spanish province. But all is not olive trees, it has also excellent arable land and rich mines. These mines have turned towns like Andújar and Linares into very important industrial centres.

What strikes the visitor most, however, are the Cazorla and Segura mountain ranges, authentical ecological refuges with splendid green landscapes, long ago gone from most of the rest of the Spanish Peninsula. So far, neither the fires nor the axe have spoilt this beauty. All sorts of wild animals and flora thrive there unaware of modern days pollution and progress. The landscapes are surprising and idyllic and in some way resemble the northen countries.

The capital, on first sight, gives us the clue of its history and progress as a city. The St. Catalina castle on top of a rocky hill, impressive and threatening, is a proof of the strategical importance of the place located always where the routes cross one another. Capital of the "Santo Reino" (Holy Kingdom) was the front line in the wars between Christians and Muslims, and later of great significance in the Napoleonic's wars. The founder of the Alhambra —Al-Amar— surrendered the city to the king Ferdinand III of Castille; this way the Castillians penetrated into both Andalucias. It was at that time when the magnificent castle —today Parador Nacional— was reconstructed. From its heights the guests dominate the panoramic view of the city and sorrounding territories. The huge Cathedral stands out from all the other buildings, with its elegant facade and thin and beautiful towers. Despite Baroque later influence, it preserves the classical Renaissance style, above all in the Sacristy, where Vandelvira achieved one the best exponents of Spanish architecture.

Translation: M.J. LOPEZ, T.D. DOBSON

Baeza. Ayuntamiento

THE TOWNS OF UBEDA
AND BAEZA

After the Navas de Tolosa Battle, the history of Andalusia took a decisive turn. The peoples from the Castillian plateau looked on a fertile, plentiful Andalusia in awe and greed.

The towns of Ubeda and Baeza had already been the subject of dispute, becoming the pillar of the "Vanguard Forces" and therefore so clearly under Castillian influence, hat today traces of Romanesque art can still be found there. The advancing forward lines provided them with the peace they needed to become firmly established in the rearguard as a bulwark of the new times.

Great and noble families strived to surpass each other in the splendour of the palaces they built on their estates, albeit medieval in style, and in the conversion of the old mosques into modern Gothic churches.

Interestingly enough, howewer, the peak of their magnificence was to come in the 16th century after the Fall of Granada, through the generosity of maecenas. Thus the town of Ubeda became an artistic and cultural centre by decision of the Secretary to Emperor Charles V, Francisco de Cobos, who could very well be considered the first Prime Minister of the Empire.

The all-embracing power fo medieval nobility, considerably restricted by the Catholic Kings, flourished anew amongst the nobles in the service of the Empire. In essence, the noble Spanish families followed the Italian example whereby the Italian nobles ruled the republics in much the same way as the Spanish nobility designed the future of the Empire.

The Vázquez de Molina Square is neither a town square nor Castillian-style public grounds, but should be considered rather as a family property giving rise to the building of a family mausoleum, instead of the town church, around the square.

Just as Charles V commissioned a funeral vault in Granada, Francisco de Cobos, whose income surpassed that of the Emperor himself, built his Pantheon Chapel of The Saviour.

While Diego de Siloé designed the Gate of Pardon in Granada's Cathedral, one of his disciples, A. de Vandelvira, took inspiration from this model for the façade of the Pantheon. He copied both the outer structure of his model, as well as the symbols present: the Arch of Triumph, allegories of Faith and Justice, great family coats of arms, mythology... all crowned by the transfiguration of Christ. He also repeated the burial layout of the Main Chapel, recreating the round chapel covered by a dome. It is interesting to note the use of unusual features that transcend the paganizing Italian influence, such as the difficult, angled sacristy door, or the curious substitution of columns by caryatids.

A. Vandelvira, an exemplary and extremely well-trained architect who was renowned for personally supervising his works, was accompanied by Janette, a decorator from Fontainbleau where feminine decoration was in full vogue. This would also explain why the sacristy is reminiscent of a French dance hall, with hanging vaults, embedded sculptures and medallions, features which Siloé and his contemporaries found unusual. Perhaps the lack of preestablished norms

Jaén. Catedral. Interior

Palacio de Jabalquinto →

BAEZA

(that the Counter Reform would later dictate) explains this exception. Trento was to set the guidelines at a later date.

The Palace of the Ortega family, known today as the National Parador of the High Constable Dávolos, stands adjacent to the Saviour, rather like a frame for it. Vandelvira also gave the façade of the nearby Palacio de las Cadenas (Palace of the Chains) is clearly of Herrerian style, however. This palace, built for Phillip II's Secretary, holds an inner courtyard (transformed into the present-day Town Hall) which is among the finest Spanish Renaissance courtyards. The sober, simple style does not at all detract from the elegance of this example of pure Renaissance style.

There were also troubled moments in Ubeda's history: Mohammed V once devastated the town; the town witnessed the fraticidal disputes between Pedro I and his step-brother; the High Constable Dávalos, a favourite of John II, was eventually persecuted here by his patron. Amongst other vicissitudes, the town opposed Cisneros and supported the Comuneros.

110 On the opposite side of the square stands the St. Mary of the Royal Fortresses Church, a clear exponent of the town's history. Here different styles blend together, ranging from Hispano-Moslem to Gothic Mudéjar, to Renaissance, to Baroque.

This is not the only example however. The Church of St. Paul, originally built as a mosque bears some Romanesque capitels, whereas the southern façade is a beautiful example of late Gothic, and the Plateresque tower reminds us of many others which look out over the Castillian plains. The same could be said of many other churches St. Isidore, St. Lawrence, St. Domenicus, Trinity Church, and so on.) which all make Ubeda a rosary of Spanish Renaissance. The innumerable palaces and stately homes from the Torres onwards: the Guadiana, Contadero, Medinilla, Montiel, Orozco or Porceles homes; provide a contrast of civil architecture to this town which certainly well deserves a visit.

The younger, twin sister", though not so richly endowed with monuments, surely does possess its own charm, making it a favourite for many. The position of the town, also standing on a hill overlooking wide, open fields, probably explains why it was the first two to be regained by the Christians (1227).

The town continually surprises the visitor with points of interest, such as the Roman Plaza de los Leones (Square of the Lions) in the town centre, surrounded by a double arch by Villalar erected in honour of Charles V, or La Casa del Populo (or People's House) and the old Carnicería (Slaughter and Tanning house), which bear witness to the town's aspiration to become a great city. Here, a simple slaughter house is adorned with one of the finest imperial coast of arms and ample windows more suited as decoration for a nobleman's house than a tannery. The Town Hall building is similar in this respect, its façade is an outstanding example of the Renaissance style (1559), although at the height of its splendour it was nothing more than the town's jail. Venturin further into the town along the narrow, medieval streets, through archways and arcades, just around one of the corners the façade of the Palacio de Jabalquinto suddenly appears, undoubtedly rivalling other buildings in Guadalajara or Salamanca in Gothic elegance. Directly opposite the Palace stands the Church of the Holy Cross-Romanesque architecture in Andalusia! Close by stands the Cathedral founded by Ferdinand III, known as Ferdinand the Saint, which was built on the foundations of a mosque. The grandiosity of the building must prove that this was the See of the bishop where Vandelvira himself worked. There are also two grilles by Master Bartholomew. The neighbouring Old University, dating from imperial times, lent its classrooms to the Spanish poet, Antonio Machado.

Convents and churches, some of which are outstanding examples of their kind, are proof of Baeza's importance as one of Spain's major historic cities.

Baeza.

Ubeda. El Salvador.

Almería. Puerto

ALMERIA

Almería is one of the eight provinces that comprise the southern part of Spain, in the region known as Andalusia. Together with the province of Cádiz, it is one of the smallest Andalusian provinces, covering an area of 8.777 square kilometres with a population of approximately 442.300 (153,600 in the capital).

The province is bathed by the Mediterranean at its southern and eastern borders; the province of Murcia lies to the north and Granada, to the west. Its lofties elevations are to be found at the Cerro de Nivar, 2.137 metres and at Picachón, 1.911 metres.

Venturing into the province from the coastline, travelling east to west, we traverse the Pulpí plains, the Sierra del Medio Mountains and finally reach the Cabezo de la Jara.

Travelling to the north, we cross the River Velez, that flows through the town of Vélez Rubio, and the River María, crossing Guadalupe. Heading westward once again, we follow the River Calar until we reach Mount Godoy, to then head south through the Collado de las Vertientes, the Sierra de Oria and lastly, the Sierras de Lucar and Baza which lead into the Sierra Nevada Mountain range. Towards the south, these ranges merge into the Alpujarra Mountains following the natural course of the River Grande for 15 kilometres, then point towards the southwest, down to the coast, through the Trebolar Hermitage.

Almeria's often rugged coastline contrast in some areas with intermittent plains. Travelling from west to east from the province of Granada, the steep coastline runs as far as the town of Adra where it levels out. Passing the two lagoons

Mojácar

found in this area, we arrive at Los Alamos which forms an inlet to accommodate the Los Baños Port. This level stretch of coast continues west as far as Punta de Elena. This swift, bird's-eye view describes the area known as the Biggt of the Almeria Gulf. Further on we find Cabo de Gata and Punta de Loma Pelada, and further still lies St. Peter's Anchorage between Punta Polacra and Punta del Plomo. The coast continues along the Vera Gulf, the Punta de Hornicos, passing the River Almanzora mouth and turning northwest to the pine forest of the Sierra de Almagrera and the San Juan de los Terreros Castle.

As early as 1500 BC, the riches of Almeria's subsoil (iron, cooper, zinc, manganese and argentiferous lead) were exploited by the ancient civilizations that once inhabited the area, and exported to the East. A great culture was founded here, with its origins in Argar (located to the north of the capital city) renowned for its pottery and ceramics production. Around the year 1000 BC, a variation of the pottery originating in this area, known as the campanulate vase, acquired surprising artistic status and is reported to have been transported over the Pyrenees, over the Alps, reaching central Europe and spreading through France to the British Isles. It is for this very reason that Professor Francisco Esteve Barba has described it as "Spain's oldest export".

Almeria's position as an outpost to the East, together with its mineral wealth and coastline, attracted the Phoenicians, the Greeks, the Romans and the Carthaginians. All along the provincial coast the Phoenicians founded their salt fisheries famous for preparing some of the culinary delights of the Mediterranean peoples.

Adra was the ancient Phoenician town of Abdera. The Romans later called it Portus Magnus or Virgitanus, perhaps because of its proximity to Virgi, today the town of Berja, Islam understood the importance of Almería, its strategic location and its potential, thus changing its name to the poetic and present-day Albaharí, or "mirror of the sea". It was under the rule of Islam that Almería saw its greatest splendour. One of the most important shipyards, the great port of "Andalus", was founded during the Moslem empire by Abderrahman III, in 995. All of the sultan's squadrons docked at this port, and the peoples of the Mediterranean towns congregated at "Andalus" with their extraordinarily beautiful and exquisite textiles that rivalled those of Baghdad.

The ancient adage:

> *When Almería was Almería.*
> *Granada was its alquería (farmstead).*

must have originated from this emporium and era of grandeur.

The Alcazaba (or Arab fortres) still remains from the days of Moslem Domain. It is perhaps Spain's most extensive military fortification, measuring 530 metres in length. The surface area within the military enclosure is highly irregular as it had to adapt to both the physical terrain and to the necessary defensive requirements inherent to the nature of the construction. The fortress is comprised of three planes arranged in decrescent fashion. The two upper planes were

built up with outbuildings for the inhabitants of the enclosure, and the third plane, at a slightly lower level, was most probably an area for gardens and where the entrance to the citadel was found.

The panorama from these heights is bound to provide a long-lasting memory. The views of the city, the sea and the gypsy district, known as La Chanca, are truly impressive.

The Christian incursions during the period of the Spanish Reconquest came unexpectedly. In 1147, Alfonso VII, aided by the King of Navarra, the Count of Barcelona and numerous knights from Genova and Pisa, conquered Almeria. Cid-Abu-Said reconquered Almería in 1157, but was later attacked by Ferdinand VI and James II of Aragon, who surrounded the city. The sultan of Granada was hence forced to sign a pact with the King of Aragon agreeing to pay 50.000 doubloons by a fixed date as well as to free all of his prisoners (January 1310). On December 22, 1489, the Catholic Monarchs seized the city, and in 1500, Pedro Fajardo had to supress a rebellion of the Morisco Spaniards.

Several treatises and dictionaries dating from the beginning of the century describe the inhabitants of Almeria as being a happy, compassionate, serious-minded yet festive and social people, with unique customs and traditions. These writings further describe them as possessing a sharp wit and keen imagination, with a natural gift for expressing themselves (however imperfect their education may have been). The regional architecture is based on buildings made primarily from stone using lime and sand rubblework. In the areas where the terrain was marly and impervious, the inhabitants made their residences in caves. Lastly, mention is made of Almeria's source of wealth —its minerals, agriculture, fisheries, marble, and export of dried fruits and grapes.

If one studies the geography of Almería on a map of Spain, the province is found in the southeastern part of the country, assuming almost a reclining posture, as though she were rocking in an easy chair. The sun bestows its first morning rays on Almería — her head proudly and nobly crowned by the Vélez Castles. The white, stately architecture has, however, been sadly and unforgivably stripped. The Sierra de las Estancias would represent her bust, while the Sierra de Filabres would be her skirt and her feet, the Sierra de Gádor, are gently bathed by the sea.

Today it comes as a surprise that Almeria is not a recognised tourist centre along with many of the other Spanish provinces occupying the southern littoral. Almería could perhaps be referred to as the Spanish Cinderella, the province that is always forgotten, happy just to gaze at the

sea and bathe in the sun, asking for nothing more. Its resources have never been fully appreciated, its potential has been forgotten, ignored, demeaned and denied the opportunity they deserve. Macael to the north has been the great, rich, white city, which has ennobled palaces, columns, capitels and churches with the luminosity of its beautiful white marble. The subsoil has lavished the entire Latin-speaking world with ist minerals. In Gádor, the north of the capital the sun has ripened a variety of orange of outstanding and exquisite qualities. Berja from its lofty heights knew of the compact, sweet grape that was shipped to the nations in Europe. Close to the sea, Adra has been renowned for centuries fot its salting industries, which were so highly esteemed by the Roman world. Its interior, having lived moments of both glory and neglect, its hills have lent their soil from prehistoric times to the present-day to fulfill the need of an agricultural people like the Spanish, as well as for today's paper industry.

This province, forever gazing at the sea from above, contemplating its mirror image in the sea — the forgotten province, has felt the physical lash of a barren land which has suffered extensive desertification. Nonetheless, many praiseworthy efforts, albeit with difficulties, have been made to restore the natural vegetation.

Almería throughout its great history has always astonished the mother land even as far back as prehistoric times. Later, Mojácar preferred to remain Moslem amidst Christian settlements. At one stage, Almería almost became a European Hollywood. The province of Almería is warmed by its own sun, boasting clear, blue skies and star-clad nights worthy of a higher realm.

The wide, open plains reaching down to the sea are, perhaps, the greatest of all the astonishing features in Almeria. the melancholic, all-embracing name given to the area, Dalías, denotes an immense, barren plain, which seems to contradict the flourishing agricultural industry of this sun-drenched land where early, greenhouse crops have produced a frequent harvest of a wide variety of fruits and vegetables, giving rise to a considerable increase in per capita income as well as a drastic reduction in unemployment.

What will Almería astonish the mother land with next? No one knows, but it certainly will be a surprise. Perhaps one day solar energy, today in its developing stages, will replace polluting forms of energy currently in use, and Almería will be able to use its trump card to change the old adage to:

When Almería is Almería
Spaing will be its alquería (farmstead)
EMILIO FUENTES LAGUNA

117

Alcazaba

La Catedral.

CADIZ

When writing about Cádiz we are obliged to use the superlative: It is in fact the most ancient city in Europe, the most southern, the most sea bound, the most liberal. etc... Because of its situation was, of old, coveted as a sheltering harbour for vessels and final destination for overseas merchandise. The harbour also served to load ships with the minerals from the province rich mines.

From the very ancient times of Tartesos or Tarteside or before —proved by the very famous anthropoid sarcophagus— later the Phoenicians days and through several other cultures up to our modern times, Cádiz has had a great sailing tradition that has stretched over 3.000 years.

It was first a Phoenician town, then a great economic Carthagenian centre; it was conquered by the Romans, Arabs and Christians (Alfonso XI in 1262) and, like a keel that goes into the sea, opened its Gates to the New World and tendered a bridge to Africa.

The English punished it from the times of Phillip II to Trafalgar. Later on it treated the French invaders with mocking contempt when besieged, and without loosing its merriness engendered the "Cortes de Cádiz" (Parliament) in 1812, a model that other European countries were to follow later.

The part of the Cádiz province situated in the Sub-Betic mountain range has white villages cattered that climb to

Parque Genovés.

La Caleta.

Puerta de Tierra

Jerez. Iglesia de San Miguel. Fachada

Jerez. Iglesia de San Miguel. Fachada

castles along tortuous, steep and narrow streets, adorned by beautiful balconies and court yards shining with white wash: Arcos de la Frontera, Ubrique, Setenil, Algodonales, Zahara, Olvera are as interesting as —difficult to explain— unknown by the tour operators. Grazalema (The rainy) —the highest village in the province— where the landscapes are so green, because of the abundant rains, a present from Heaven in these latitudes; a very interesting variety of pine tree (Pinsapo) grows there. It has also a very rich fauna which includes all sorts of wild animals.

The traveller must visit Medina Sidonia a town of ancient lineage, or Vejer, white and high like a pigeons nest. From there starts the fighting bull country to near the Gibraltar area, going through Tarifa (The loyal) without forgetting the small lake of La Janda, so important in Spanish history, The Carbonera mountain range, Los Barrios, Algeciras, with its important port, San Roque (the proud) all without loosing sight of the Rock.

Cádiz is surrounded by sea towns: San Fernando, Los Astilleros, Las Salinas, La Bahía but above all the Puerto de Santa María and Jerez. This is the zone of the internationally most known wines; and well deserves this fame. From here to San Lucar the wine "Bodegas" (Vaults) perfume the air lifting up the spirits with their penetrating aroma. Bacus would not wish another Olimpo. The whitish lands and the Atlantic winds engender here the best "Manzanilla" (Light sherry) in the world. Jerez is, besides, the cradle of the Spanish horse (Cartujano). La Cartuja is an outstanding architectural work. La Colegiata, San Miguel, San Marcos or the Ponce de León palace are, together with the Castle, remains of a glorious past.

The making of sherry is a rather misterious myth. The harvest takes place early, in September. After the grapes have been laid in the sun and the grape juice obtained, this ferments under rigorous surveillance; after it is drawn out, cleaned and poured into big casks made of American oak wood. All this is done with the care these exquisite wines deserve, but surprisingly every cask makes different wines. Even if the chemical component are the same and the casks adjoining one another, only the fine sense of smell of the "Bodeguero" (Cellarer) light and dry of pale shades, or an "Amontillado" which will be kept longer in the cask, up to an excellent "Palo cortado". It could also be an "Oloroso" completely different from the others or a sweet unsurpassable Pedro Ximénez.

González Byass

Jerez.
La Colegiata.

All of it constitutes a chain of work where not a single link can fail, and helped by the passing of time, complete the almost miraculous achievement.

Translation: M.J. LOPEZ, T.D. DOBSON

La Cartuja. Fachada

Olvera.

Zahara de la Sierra

La Rábida

La Rábida

Huelva. Monumento a Colón

HUELVA

The Sierra Morena serves as a link between the central tableland and Andalucía. Across this spine, Andalusia sinks its roots in northern Spain, unseen, to appear afterwards in the south by a blue sea with golden sands.

Huelva, in western Andalusia, is a good example. It is almost Extremadura in the Sierra de Arcana when the white villages abound between green forests of chestnut, oak and holm oak. It is to these latter that the Iberian pigs go to eat the acorns which are responsible for producing the hams of Jabugo, the best ham in the world. And there also, scattered like doves are the villages of Alajar, and authentic jewel of ethnic architecture, lost in solitude, Aroche, enclosed in medieval walls, Almonstar, more known for its fandango dances than for its mosque, (probably the best preserved mosque of Spain outside Córdoba), Cortigana and many other.

In addition to white and green, the third colour of the northern part of Andalusia, is ochre, the rust-coloured earth telling us that more reserves of iron exist. For this mineral, civilizations have entered here since antiquity.

The river Guadiana borders Huelva on the west, as do the streams which flow down from the mountains and flow over the Andalucian lowlands and into the salt marsh. This is the marsh bordering three pearls, Rábida in Palos where Columbus revealed the adventures of his discovery, Moguer which sings of heroes and poets, and medieval Niebla. Everywhere here is sand, pine and eucalyptus trees and here, also is the nature reserve fed by the Guadalquivir river.

Its outlook is so Andalucian that it treasures in its heart none other than the Virgen del Rocío. All the world envies her for the miracle of the Doñana, but Andalusia envies her for the "White Dove". The phenomenon of the cult of the Virgen del Rocío is unique. It has been attempted to explain its origens in the pagan festival of spring, or the triumph of ranches over farming and to look for justification for its superstitions there, but there is much more than an ethnic-roots phenomenon in popular feeling. How can they wrong when it is so emphatically popular? The pilgrimage of the Virgen acts as a catalyst for a profound collective religious feeling which is also a way of life and of understanding life. There is no possible comparison and it is difficult to understand for one who does not participate in the faith that moves it.

The Atlantic breeze, the scent of the nature reserve, the horses, the water, and the pastures give this Andalusia a special and unequaled air of open spirit and a cosmopolitan soul.

126

Almonaster La Real

Segura de la Sierra